OF THESE EMBLEMS

OF THESE EMBLEMS

S. Michael Wilcox • Joy Saunders Lundberg • E. Douglas Clark
Toni Sorenson • Hank Smith • Margaret McConkie Pope
Brent L. Top • Mary Jane Woodger

Covenant Communications, Inc.

Cover image: *Sacrament Bread and Water* © Intellectual Reserve, Inc.

Cover design © 2010 by Covenant Communications, Inc.

Published by Covenant Communications, Inc.
American Fork, Utah

Printed in Canada
First Printing: September 2010

16 15 14 13 12 11 10   10 9 8 7 6 5 4 3 2 1

ISBN: 978-1-59811-706-6

$\mathscr{T}$ABLE OF CONTENTS

*I*NTRODUCTION

E VERY WEEK, FAITHFUL LATTER-DAY SAINTS come from all walks of life and from every circumstance to sup at the Lord's table, to partake of the sacrament and thus renew covenants made in the waters of baptism. We come each week, our spirits—and sometimes our bodies—battered and broken by the extremities of life. There, in communion with our fellow-citizens in the kingdom, we bow our heads and offer up our broken hearts, our contrite spirits—our desire to do better, to be better. And in that singular ordinance we are offered the chance indeed to be better—with a sure promise that after all we can do, He will make up the difference.

Though in fulfillment of prophecy not a single bone of His body was broken during His exquisitely difficult ordeal for us, there is great meaning in the fact that the sacramental loaf must be broken. For it is only when we approach the sacrament table with broken hearts that we are able to fully partake.

In the prayer we are coaxed—no, commanded—to remember. *Remember.* As our minds soar across the millennia, we find there is so much to remember about Him that we in turn should exemplify ourselves. We remember His love for *all*—not just the attractive or powerful or wealthy or righteous. We remember His desire to do the Father's will always—not just when it was convenient or easy. We remember the battle against evil that He waged in Gethsemane and that He fought until He won—no matter the cost. And we remember His complete devotion to righteousness. We remember, and we offer our own hearts, trusting Him to be with us every step of the way.

As we wait reverently, the emblems are passed to each one there assembled. Every one has the opportunity to partake, for in the Lord's kingdom, not a single one is overlooked. Each is invited. Through some infinite eternal arithmetic that our mere mortal minds cannot grasp, the power of the Savior's Atonement reaches out to touch us in a unique way, carried tenderly by deacons—the smallest and weakest, for those moments each Sunday made strong enough to help deliver salvation.

In our partaking, we remember Him, and we anxiously hope to become acceptable. In our weekly taking of the emblems of His flesh and blood, we are helped in that quest, becoming clean once again. And we do remember Him. For Him, the cup was bitter—the most anguished any has ever been asked to sip. Had it been up to Him, and Him alone—had not innumerable souls hung in the balance, had not He stood unwavering in that great and crowning council—perhaps He would have turned from that bitter cup with its horrific dregs. But it was not up to Him alone, because His very life—His will, His purpose, all that He was—reflected in perfect oneness the will of the Father whose Son He was. And so, exercising every fiber of His remarkable strength and courage, He drank of that bitter cup so that we would not have to. Instead, the cup from which we drink each week is clean and pure—quenching manna to our hungry spirits, yearning to be fed by all that He is.

When the cool, clear water touches our lips, we might remember that His experience was far different. Exhausted, bruised, His flesh torn, He hung in agony and must have trembled with a thirst unlike any we could know. No relief came—only a sponge soaked in acrid vinegar was pressed to His parched lips—until He gave up the ghost and declared, "It is finished" (John 19:30).

Throughout the history of mankind, there have been singular moments of pure communion between mortal and Deity, moments to which we have been afforded a glimpse through holy writ. There was Moses and the burning bush. There was the brother of Jared and the sixteen stones. There was the boy Joseph entering the grove of trees. And if we bring to the table a sufficiently broken heart and a sufficiently contrite spirit, we can find in the administration of the sacrament our own sacred grove . . . our own singular moment of pure communion with the divine.

We live in difficult times—times that try the mettle of even the most courageous and strong. Even as we feel ready to lose faith in the battle, we are brought to Him . . . given a chance through partaking of the symbols of His flesh and blood to grasp renewed faith, to cling to fresh hope. For as we hear His promise to always be with us, we remember that He bids us to "be of good cheer" (John 16:33). And it occurs to us that of all people, we have the most to be cheerful about. And so we leave the sacramental table each week filled with not only courage for the battle, but joy in the process . . . the cheer He so mercifully gives us.

OF THESE EMBLEMS
By S. Michael Wilcox

MY FIRST REAL MEMORY OF the sacrament occurred when I was about eight or nine. While I had partaken of the sacrament from my earliest childhood, this was the first time its power settled into me and changed me in a profound manner. During sacrament meeting I always sat right next to my mother so she could keep an eye on me, and I could hear her sing the hymns; she had sung professionally earlier in her life, and her voice was beautiful. I was usually not too interested in what was going on, and I was restlessly eager to escape the confining restrictions of the pews. But this particular Sunday was different.

The hymn the chorister selected to prepare the congregation for the sacrament was "More Holiness Give Me." As was my habit, I did not sing—but as my mother began to sing, a feeling descended upon me that I had not experienced before. It was warm, inviting, laced with joy, and overflowing with peace. I listened intently to the words of the hymn. I understood them on a level beyond my young years.

My mother's voice penetrated into places in my soul that had been somewhat vacant until that Sunday evening. By *vacant* I don't mean empty; instead, they were reserved for those things of deep import of which I was, until this time, largely unaware. Now the emptiness filled and the words hung in that silent place heavily and radiantly.

I particularly recall the impact of the line "more longing for home." I realized that the world, with all its little-boy wonders that I so enjoyed, was not really home—I suddenly knew that there was a more beautiful place of which I had no memory. I was filled with homesickness, a longing for a distant landscape and, perhaps more important, for family members who dwelled there. I was raised by my mother and my two sisters; I did not have a father or brother, but the yearning encompassed a Father and a Brother.

My mother continued to sing the lyrics that had suddenly become so vital to me. The last words of the hymn drifted to me: "more Savior like thee." I loved Jesus at that moment, purely and with childlike innocence. There was born in my heart through the soothing words of my mother's voice the desire to be like Him. At that moment, while the priests reverently broke the bread, the reality of my life's mission came home to me in a most earnest way, and I knew what I needed to do—what I *wanted* to do. I knew that the key to returning to my eternal home was to be like Jesus.

When the meeting was over we went home. I sensed I needed to be alone, so I climbed into the branches of the large elm tree in our front yard. I can still feel the green coolness around me and see the filtered sunlight penetrating my hiding place. There I sang quietly to myself, over and over, the words of "More Holiness Give Me." I thought of home and of Jesus. Such is the power and the promise of the sacrament!

During our time away from our heavenly home, we need occasionally to reconnect with its spirit. I believe deeply that a wise Father in Heaven understood that and provided means, very simple means, for us to feel the consolations and encouragement of the Spirit. In my own life I know that when I need to breathe heavenly air there are five places I can find it: on my knees in prayer, in the pages of the scriptures, in the beauty and solitude of the natural world, within the walls of the temple, and in the ordinance of the sacrament. Though the intensity of the encounter with the Spirit varies, these five never fail me. I'd like to explore a few ideas about one of those—the ordinance of the sacrament.

The Bread and Water: Overcoming the Two Deaths

I USED TO WONDER WHY the sacrament involved two symbols— wouldn't one be sufficient to remind us of the Savior's gift? It took a number of years before I realized there was wonderful symbolism in the use of both bread and water, and that the associated symbolism had a deeper meaning than the Savior's body and blood.

As a result of the Fall, two deaths entered the world— spiritual and physical. Because man is subject to spiritual death, we are cut off from the presence of the Father; because of physical death, our spirits leave our mortal bodies when our time in mortality is finished. Both are in a certain manner catastrophic. Our spirits long for eternal union with God as well as eternal union with our physical bodies. That these unions may be everlasting, Christ came into the world. Each symbol of the sacrament reminds us of Jesus' victory over both deaths—the bread a reminder of His victory over physical death, the water a reminder of His victory over spiritual death.

Doctrine and Covenants 27 helps us see the distinction between the two symbols. While on his way to procure the emblems of the sacrament, Joseph Smith received the revelation recorded in Section 27 that gives instruction regarding the sacrament. Notice what the Lord says: "I say unto you, that it mattereth not what ye shall eat or what ye shall drink when ye partake of the sacrament, if it so be that ye do it with an eye single to my glory—remembering unto the Father *my body which was laid down for you, and my blood which was shed for the remission of your sins*" (D&C 27:2, emphasis added).

The last part of this verse indicates the two main things Christ did for us that we are to remember. Jesus laid down His body that He might take it up again and thus bring to us all the gift of the Resurrection. He also shed His blood that we might receive a remission of our sins through the compassion and mercy of the Atonement.

We sense this same distinction when the Savior taught the Nephites and Lamanites at the temple in Bountiful. There was one emblem for the Resurrection and one for the Atonement. When teaching about the bread, the Savior told the people they were to administer the bread "unto all those who shall believe and be baptized in my name. . . . And this shall ye do in *remembrance of my body, which I have shown unto you*" (3 Ne. 18:5, 7, emphasis added).

The body He had shown them was His resurrected body.

For the longest time during the quiet moments of the sacrament, I focused my thoughts on the broken body of

Christ on the cross. This is certainly an appropriate way of approaching the sacrament. Paul, when speaking of the ordinance of the sacrament, reminded the Corinthian Saints of the Savior's actions and words during the Last Supper: "The Lord Jesus the same night in which he was betrayed took bread: And when he had given thanks, he brake it, and said, Take, eat: this is my body, which is broken for you: this do in remembrance of me" (1 Cor. 11:23–24). It is easy to see the positioning of the words "took bread and . . . brake it" with "this is my body which is broken for you."

To the Nephites a different emphasis is explained that gives added insight and deeper meaning to the sacrament. It seems in Christ's own instructions it is the living, eternal, glorified, resurrected body we are to think of as much as, if not more than, the broken body. We continue to ponder the broken body, but we miss part of the essential goodness of this ordinance if we fail to ponder the resurrected body. We all have or will at some future time experience the death of someone we love. These can be very painful times, but there is hope, comfort, and consolation in the sacrament, knowing that those we miss will one day rise from the grave glorified as Christ is glorified. The sacrament was given to us to keep this hope before our eyes every week. That hope comes from a "remembrance of my body which I have shown unto you."

Having given the multitude the bread of His Resurrection, He now turned to the wine of His atoning blood. When they had partaken of the wine, Jesus said, "This shall ye always do to those who *repent* and are baptized in my name; and ye shall do it in remembrance of my blood, which I have shed for you" (3 Ne. 18:11, emphasis added). Repenting and being baptized are the key points in this part of the ordinance, repentance being necessary that the blood of the Lamb may cleanse and purify us.

As we partake of the sacrament we are invited to ponder, receive hope, and be comforted by the twin thoughts of Christ's dual victory over the two deaths. Each is critical to our eternal happiness. Depending on what we are experiencing in our lives on any given Sunday, one may be more vital than the other, but they are equally powerful. There have been times when I am faced with the uncertainty of life or the death of one I love; at those times, I am deeply grateful as I partake of the bread. On other occasions the weakness of the flesh and its propensity to stray dominates my thoughts and I take courage and hope in the water, knowing I can be cleansed just as water is the prime cleansing agent of life.

The Bread of Life and the Living Water

SYMBOLS ARE POWERFUL FOR A number of reasons, not least of which is their ability to suggest many truths to the mind. Though the main idea of the bread and water is the conquest of death and sin, other ideas may be equally powerful as we reflect on the Savior during the sacrament.

In the synagogue at Capernaum, Jesus proclaimed, "I am the bread of life: he that cometh to me shall never hunger. . . . Your fathers did eat manna in the wilderness, and are dead. This is the bread which cometh down from heaven, that a man may eat thereof, and not die. I am the living bread which came down from heaven" (John 6:35, 49–51).

Bread is the staff of life; so too may we be fed spiritually by our Savior's teachings. We need only contemplate the nourishing power of the Prodigal Son story or the Sermon on the Mount to understand how the human spirit is filled.

Jesus spoke of "living water" often during His ministry. To the woman at the well in Samaria He offered this living water, saying, "Whosoever drinketh of the water that I shall give him shall never thirst; but the water that I shall give him shall be in him a well of water springing up into everlasting life" (John 4:14). On the Temple Mount in Jerusalem, He offered the living water of His spirit and His message to all who thirsted: "Jesus stood and cried, saying, If any man thirst, let him come unto me, and drink . . . as the scripture hath said, out of his belly shall flow rivers of living water" (John 7:37–38).

The sacrament may also remind us that Jesus is the main source of spiritual nourishment. We need His teachings and His example of living just as we need bread and water. Without them we physically perish. Without the Bread of Life and the Living Water, we spiritually perish. Jesus promised that those who partook of the sacrament would be filled: "He that eateth this bread eateth of my body to his soul; and he that drinketh of this wine drinketh of my blood to his soul; and his soul shall never hunger nor thirst, but shall be filled." The promise was immediately realized, for "when the multitude had all eaten and drunk, behold, they were filled with the spirit" (3 Ne. 20:8–9).

The Bitter Cup

WE CAN FIND FURTHER EDIFICATION in our thoughts during the sacrament by understanding the bitter cup

Jesus drank for all of us. We drink a cup to remember His cup. He spoke of that cup when He introduced Himself to the waiting multitude at the temple in Bountiful: "I am the light and the life of the world, and I have drunk out of that bitter cup which the Father hath given me" (3 Ne. 11:11). Jesus' own inclusion of the bitter cup in His introduction suggests He would have us remember it.

In scripture, we are given an image of the Atonement we can visualize. When Jesus prayed in the Garden of Gethsemane He used the metaphor of the cup in His plea to His Father: "And he went a little further, and fell on his face, and prayed, saying, O my Father, if it be possible, let this cup pass from me: nevertheless not as I will, but as thou wilt" (Matt. 26:39).

As Jesus approached His "hour" and entered Gethsemane, Matthew tells us He "began to be sorrowful and very heavy. Then saith he unto them, My soul is exceeding sorrowful, even unto death" (Matt. 26:37–38). Mark expresses that Jesus "began to be sore amazed, and to be very heavy" (Mark 14:33). Even the God of the galaxy could be amazed by the weight of human suffering—a greater load than even He had thought.

The cup was bitter indeed, and He shrank from the trembling. But the cup needed to be drained, so in accordance to His Father's will and against His own poignant pleading, He began to drink. He drank it throughout His moments in Gethsemane. He drank it during the trials before the Jewish leaders. He drank it during His examination before both Pilate and Herod. He drank it during the scourging and on the cross. There then came a moment on the cross when He made a simple, single request for Himself: "I thirst" (John 19:28).

A sponge was dipped into a vessel filled with vinegar and given to Jesus. "When Jesus therefore had received the vinegar, he said, It is finished: and he bowed his head, and gave up the ghost" (John 19:30). Luke tells us that "the soldiers also mocked him, coming to him, and offering him vinegar" (Luke 23:36). This mocking offer of bitterness is best described in Psalms, where in a certain way we are given the Savior's own view of the vinegar from the cross: "Reproach hath broken my heart; and I am full of heaviness: and I looked for some to take pity, but there was none; and for comforters, but I found none. They gave me also gall for my meat; and in my thirst they gave me vinegar to drink" (Ps. 69:20–21). At that moment Jesus knew He had drained the bitter cup to the last. It was finished, and He returned to His Father.

Each Sabbath we are invited to drink a cup to remember and honor He who drank a cup much more bitter. A cup for a cup! Somehow it is all so fitting. We then have much we can ponder during those few minutes each week when the bread and the water move throughout the congregation. Each thought has the power to fill us with both gratitude and hope and keep the sacrament from becoming, because of its frequency, a moment much like every other.

A Testimonial—An Examination—A Communion

THERE ARE FEW PLACES IN scripture where the sacrament is explained with more comprehension than in 1 Corinthians as taught by the Apostle Paul. The Corinthian Saints had instituted practices that were compromising the sacred nature of the sacrament, and Paul wrote to correct their beliefs.

Paul spoke of the sacrament as constituting four different things. We have already spoken of one—the sacrament is a memorial of both gratitude and hope. Having affirmed this most essential of aspects, Paul then wrote: "For as often as ye eat this bread, and drink this cup, ye do shew the Lord's death till he come" (1 Cor. 11:26). A quick glance at the footnote next to the word *shew* gives us additional words from the Greek that add dimension to the verb chosen by Paul. To *shew* the Lord's death means to "proclaim" or "announce" something—to testify of it.

In this manner the sacrament is a testimonial.

If I were to ask a group of Latter-day Saints how many Sundays a month are testimony Sundays, they would answer "one." The proper answer is that every Sunday is testimony Sunday—every time we take the sacrament, we are proclaiming and announcing to the world with an outward act that we believe Jesus is the Christ. We affirm His Resurrection. We attest to His atoning sacrifice. We say to all who care to witness that we have faith in Christ, desire to take His name, want to remember Him, and are striving to keep His commandments. We proclaim to all that we need His Spirit to be with us and that we are asking for it.

Such testimony arises from the depths of the soul. As we partake of the bread and drink the cup of water, we testify to all present, "Jesus is my Lord. My hope and happiness rest in His compassion and sacrifice."

That is the testimony. Now let's look at the examination. Paul next tells the Corinthians of the need to turn inward and ponder one's worthiness as the sacrament approaches. "Let a man examine himself, and so let him eat of that bread, and drink of that cup. . . . For if we would judge ourselves, we should not be judged" (1 Cor. 11:28, 31). If we fail to do this self-assessment, Paul indicates, we are "not discerning the Lord's body" (v. 29).

The word *examine* can also mean "prove." We bring to the Lord the proof that we are worthy to partake of the emblems that represent His Atonement, but we also prove ourselves in the assurance that we understand the significance of what we do. We examine ourselves; we find those things we have done, are doing, or are failing to do; and we acknowledge to the Lord that we will try even more earnestly to live as He lived. Since this is a high ideal, one that often is beyond our mortal grasp, the Lord has given us an ordinance that recognizes our need to weekly recommit and weekly receive forgiveness for our humanity and our failures.

For most of us, *examination* and *judge* are not the most positive words. In this case, however, the words are not meant to be threatening, but inviting. Judging ourselves implies we realize our true condition, a condition that humbly needs the Savior's mercy. Paul is not suggesting a harsh self-scrutiny, but a meek requesting. If we find we do need the forgiving compassion of the Savior and we are willing to continue in our efforts to be constantly worthy of His Spirit and His forgiveness, we will be accepted by Him. We leave the sacrament table as clean and spotless as we were the day we were baptized.

That is the examination. And what of the communion?

Because the word *communion* is used by other religions, we are not always comfortable applying it to our own ordinance of the sacrament. However, it is a perfectly acceptable word and carries most significant meaning. Paul wrote the Corinthians, "The cup of blessing which we bless, is it not the communion of the blood of Christ? The bread which we break, is it not the communion of the body of Christ? For we being many are one bread, and one body: for we are all partakers of that one bread" (1 Cor. 10:16–17).

Once again the footnote is helpful. The Greek suggests for *communion* the words *aid, fellowship,* and *partnership.* There are two types of communion or fellowship inherent in the sacrament—that of us with Christ, His Father, and the Holy Spirit, and that of love and unity with each other. The sacrament was designed to create and foster both unities.

There is a natural power in the sacrament that brings us closer to the Savior and to His Father, just as I experienced as a child listening to my mother sing the sacrament hymn. There is also a facility in the sacrament to create oneness between us as part of God's family. When I served as a bishop I was overcome numerous times by how much love I felt for the members of the ward as I looked into their faces during the sacrament. Impressions would come more easily during that time, and I often knew which members I needed to talk with.

For those who struggle with bitter feelings or are struggling to forgive another, I have discovered that the sacrament can be wonderfully powerful in minimizing those negative emotions. During that quiet reflective time it is easier to say with Jesus, "Father forgive them [as I forgive them], for they know not what they do" (Luke 23:34). We cannot always hold those soft feelings in our hearts. The anger may seep back into our souls during the week, but we return on Sunday to the sacrament and once again can feel the refreshing liberation of bitterness draining away. The sacrament as a communion of hearts and minds is thus needful in creating the Zion society we are striving to bring into existence, where all will be "of one heart and one mind" not only with each other, but with God (see Moses 7:18).

Section 27 of the Doctrine and Covenants is perhaps one of the best places to search for the meaning of the sacrament as a communion, for it speaks of a grand communion to which we are all invited. "The hour cometh," Jesus teaches, "that I will drink of the fruit of the vine with you on the earth and with Moroni . . . And also with Elias . . . And also John the son of Zacharias . . . And also Elijah . . . And also with Joseph and Jacob, and Isaac, and Abraham . . . And also with Michael . . . and also with Peter, and James, and John . . . *And also with all those whom my Father hath given me out of the world*" (D&C 27:5–14, emphasis added).

What a glorious truth this offers. We too are invited to that supper of suppers where, in the presence of Christ Himself and all those who taught of Him, we will reflect on the great plan of happiness and the sacrifice that made it all possible. What will it be like to sing one of the sacramental hymns with the Savior there in body as He was always there in Spirit when we partook of the emblems of His love?

Each Sabbath we are invited to make the sacrament one of the most spiritual moments of the week—a refreshing, strengthening, quickening time. We can prevent the sacrament from becoming commonplace by pondering the sacrament's different elements and purposes from week to week. We are still walking the narrow path; we still ask for help and forgiveness, we are preparing to make the judgment both a pleasing and simple experience.

To Hold a Place within His Heart: Always Remember He Does Not Remember

WE GENERALLY THINK OF THE sacrament as an ordinance that instills the Savior deeply and comfortably with our hearts, but it is also a reminder that we hold a loving place within His heart. It is a memorial that allows us to enter into Him as He enters into us.

That holy place in His heart does not savor our past misdeeds, nor does it have room for the memory of sin. It holds only the noble and the good—not darkness, not even faint traces of divine disappointment. In our turning to Him, the past we often struggle so painfully to forget fades out of His heart as mist on a summer day.

There is a sweet assurance in the words of Isaiah that is phrased in terms of the offerings and sacrifices encompassed in the Mosaic Law, but it is not hard to make it relevant to our own times. The Savior starts this section of Isaiah by declaring, "This people have I formed for myself; they shall shew forth my praise" (Isa. 43:21). Though the Lord anticipated that His people would glorify Him before the world, they have been less than enthusiastic about the prospect. Their forms of worship have been lightly given, even though the Lord has not required of them difficult things nor burdened them with heavy commandments. He reminds them of this and then tells us what the people brought to Him instead:

"But thou hast not called upon me, O Jacob; but thou has been weary of me, O Israel. Thou hast not brought me the small cattle of thy burnt offerings; neither hast thou honored me with thy sacrifices. I have not caused thee to serve with an offering, nor wearied thee with incense. Thou hast bought me no sweet cane with money, neither hast thou filled me with the fat of thy sacrifices" (Isa. 43:22–24).

Two key words in this passage are *serve* and *weary.* The idea is the same as that in the hymn, "How Gentle God's Commands" (*Hymns,* No. 125). The same truth is expressed when we sing, "Sweet is the Work" (*Hymns,* No. 147). In John's first epistle he told the early Saints, "we [must] keep his commandments: and his commandments are not grievous" (1 John 5:3).

Though the Lord had not wearied His people or caused them to serve under burdensome commands, they had wearied Him and caused Him to serve under a heavy burden. Isaiah continues the Lord's words: "But thou hast made me to serve with thy sins, thou hast wearied me with thine iniquities" (Isa. 43:24).

God wanted sacrifice, prayer, worship, and gratitude to be laid upon the altar of His love, but instead He received the sins, weaknesses, and follies of the people. What will He do with these unasked-for offerings? The Lord answers with characteristic mercy and gentleness: "I, even I, am he that blotteth out thy transgressions for mine own sake, and will not remember thy sins" (Isa. 43:25). In humility and love He acknowledges the sins of the people, but with the firm assurance that those past deeds will not hinder His future relationship with us. He will not remember the past transgressions. He asks only

one thing of His people for the bounty of His patience
and compassion: "Put me in remembrance: let us plead
together" (Isa. 43:26).

The positioning of the words *not remember* and *put
me in remembrance* is profoundly beautiful. We are to
remember that He does not remember. Therein we may
always have hope.

In a very similar manner, the Lord asks of us our
devotion, prayers, hymns, temple observance, and other
forms of worship. We surely bring this to Him week
by week, but we also bring our sins to the altar of our
prayers. Yet, as He did with ancient Israel, He accepts
both the negative with the positive. He takes the sins,
allowing us to go free and clean. All He asks is that we
remember His non-remembrance. If we are to continue
to feel confidence in the presence of the Lord, if we
are to feel comfortable in our daily conversations, it is
imperative and necessary that we fully believe the message
of Isaiah 43.

The assurance that He does not remember is taught
repeatedly in scripture. Ezekiel wrote: "If the wicked . . .
do that which is lawful and right, he shall surely live. . . .
All his transgressions that he hath committed, they shall
not be mentioned unto him: in his righteousness that
he hath done he shall live" (Ezek. 18:21). The Lord also
told Isaiah He knew that He must forgive and forget the
failings of His people, "for the spirit should fail before
me, and the souls which I have made" (Isa. 57:16).

In our own dispensation these same truths were
emphasized by the Lord when He testified, "I, the Lord,
remember them no more" (D&C 58:42). In partaking
of the sacrament we acknowledge the reality of the

Lord's non-remembrance. For us to continue our quest for perfection, this truth must be constantly before our minds. We must, indeed, always remember Him, for His memory of our failings is short indeed.

May the private and pivotal moments we spend with our Savior each week bring the consolation, encouragement, forgiveness, and hope we all need, until that day when we all partake of the sacrament with Him in the kingdom of our Father in Heaven. On that day we will no longer need a memorial to His sacrifice and our love, for we will see Him face-to-face, witness the testifying wounds of redemption, and share with Him eternal joy in the presence of His God and our God, His Father and our Father.

ℙARTAKE AND BE FILLED
By Joy Saunders Lundberg

SOMETIMES A SACRAMENT MEETING SPEAKER will say something that lingers in your mind for years to come. That happened to me when a speaker was giving a talk about the importance of the sacrament. He told about a man who came into a meeting and sat on the pew beside him; he didn't recognize the man and found out later he was not a member of the Church. The man was attentive and reverent. When the sacrament bread was passed the man took a piece and said in a barely audible voice, "Thank you, Jesus." When the water was passed, he drank and again said, "Thank you, Jesus." The speaker told how touched he was by this man's gratitude to the Savior for what He had done for him.

Now whenever I partake of the sacrament I often find myself thinking the words, "Thank you, Jesus." Expressing gratitude in our hearts for what the Savior has done for us is significantly important; however, that is just one part of the sacrament experience for Latter-day Saints.

Elder Joseph Anderson explained, "When we enter into the waters of baptism we enter into covenant with the Lord that we will keep the commandments that He has given us. When we partake of the sacrament we renew that covenant; we partake of these emblems in remembrance of the atoning sacrifice of our Lord and Savior; we express a willingness to take upon us His name, the name of our Lord and Master, our Savior, Jesus Christ; and we covenant that we will always remember Him, that we will keep the commandments which He has given us" ("We Are a Covenant-making People," *Ensign,* Nov. 1976, 89).

In speaking about the sacrament, Elder Jeffrey R. Holland reminded us that we as a people need to take the sacrament much more seriously than we often do—and that the sacrament is the real purpose of sacrament meeting, not something to rush through so we can get on with the rest of the meeting. He also counseled that everything in the meeting, all that is spoken or sung, should be in harmony with that sacred ordinance (see "'This Do in Remembrance of Me,'" *Ensign,* Nov. 1995, 67).

When the Savior introduced the sacrament to His disciples after His resurrection, as recorded in Third Nephi, he commanded them to "bring forth some bread and wine unto him. . . . And when the Disciples had come with bread and wine, he took of the bread and brake and blessed it; and he gave unto the Disciples and commanded that they should eat. And when they had eaten and were filled, he commanded that they should give unto the multitude.

"And when the multitude had eaten and were filled, he said unto the Disciples: Behold there shall one be ordained among you, and to him will I give power that he shall break bread and bless it and give it unto the people of my church, unto all those who shall believe and be baptized in my name. And this shall ye always observe to do, even as I have done, even as I have broken bread and blessed it and given it unto you. And this shall ye do in remembrance of my body, which I have shown unto you. And it shall be a testimony unto the Father that ye do always remember me. And if ye do always remember me ye shall have my Spirit to be with you" (3 Ne. 18:1, 3–7).

He repeated the same process when administering and serving the wine: "And it came to pass that they did so, and did drink of it and were filled; and they gave unto the multitude, and they did drink, and they were filled" (3 Ne. 18:9).

What does it mean to be *filled?* What is it that makes partaking of the sacrament a fulfilling experience for members of the Church? Is our faith sufficient to enjoy the fulfillment the Lord has waiting for us?

The key may be in always remembering Him wherever we may be, and especially during this sacred ordinance. If we do this, He promises that "ye shall have my Spirit to be with you" (3 Ne. 18:11). To have His Spirit with us may be precisely what it means to *be filled.*

Learning to Be Filled

I REMEMBER SACRAMENT MEETINGS YEARS ago when our five children were small. It was a challenge to stay focused and to feel the Spirit as they wriggled and poked each other, too-loudly asking, "When will the snackerment come?" Some Sundays I felt sufficiently righteous just getting them ready enough to show up. For several of those years I was the task master while my bishopric husband sat on the stand, smiling encouragement from afar. Now I see young mothers and fathers doing the same

thing—trying their best. I have learned that "their best"
—or close to it—is good enough for those challenging
years.

How glad I am that we didn't let the difficultness of
it keep us away. There were moments scattered here and
there throughout those years that made it all worthwhile.
Those children understand it now as they experience
the same with their little ones. And I've also discovered
that finding the sacrament to be an anticipated delicious
"snack" isn't too far off base. Gradually the deliciousness
takes on new meaning, with feelings of joy and renewal.

We can experience this joy of having His Spirit
with us in a variety of ways. In sharing her sacrament
experience, a friend told me, "One Sunday as the priests
tore the bread I pondered *Why do they tear the bread?* At
that moment the hymn rang out in my mind—'bruised,
broken, torn for us'—and a picture came to me of Jesus
with His arms outstretched, the spikes being driven
through His hands and His flesh tearing. At that moment
the Spirit enveloped me, and I knew of His love for me.
The experience of taking the sacrament has ever been
changed by that moment."

Along this same line, a priesthood holder shared
this experience: "As in most wards the youth prepare
and administer the sacrament, but occasionally the
Melchizedek Priesthood has the privilege of administering
the sacrament. I was fortunate because I often had the
privilege of blessing the sacrament. During the sacrament
hymn as we broke the bread, with each tear of a piece
of bread my heart seemingly broke as I thought of the
agony of the Garden, each lash of the scourging, the
tearing of flesh from the nails, and the precious blood of

the Savior flowing. I knelt with tears in my eyes and with all the tenderness of my heart to bless the bread or water. At these times, the sacrament became even more sacred to me. Now whenever I watch a priesthood holder break bread, my heart remembers and swells with love for my Savior, the Lord Jesus Christ."

The Power of Sacrament Hymns

As these stories have testified, there is something deeply touching about the sacrament hymns. Singing them and hearing the congregation sing them always helps me prepare my mind and heart for the sacrament. They are like an official invitation that opens the door for the Spirit—even for angels—to attend the meeting and bring comfort to our souls. Many times I have felt the Spirit so powerfully during the singing that my tears can't be restrained. We all come seeking His forgiveness and the sweet assurance that He is with us and will help us with our trials. Sacrament hymns help that happen for me.

The following account gives a glimpse into the feelings of those who suffer from sin so serious that they are denied the opportunity of partaking of the sacrament. A member wrote the following experience of the blessing of a sacrament hymn during his time of repentance:

> Nearly a decade ago I went to my bishop and confessed some terrible sins that would lead to my excommunication several weeks later. As I sat in sacrament meeting the next week, and we sang the sacrament hymn, "Gently Raise the Sacred Strain"

(*Hymns,* No. 146), the words of the fourth verse struck home with me:

> Holy, holy is the Lord.
> Precious, precious is his word:
> Repent and live,
> Repent and live;
> Tho your sins be crimson red,
> Oh, repent, and he'll forgive.
> Oh, repent, and he'll forgive.

I am a seventh-generation member of the Church and have sung or heard this hymn my entire life, but never did it have the impact that it did at that time. Tears flowed as I thought of the ordeal ahead, of the sweet feelings of release and forgiveness that I might feel later on, and of the Savior's love for me.

Fourteen months later, I was rebaptized, and am again able to partake of the life-giving sacrament. The words "Oh repent, and he'll forgive" are in my mind and heart each time I partake of the bread and water, and I feel His grace in my life.

Being Worthy to Partake

Another brother wrote, "I will always remember the day I was sitting next to my good friend, who had been excommunicated, as the sacrament was being passed that day. I cannot describe the feeling of grief I experienced that day as I partook of the sacrament knowing how my friend must have felt as he held the tray for me, not being permitted to partake himself.

"I still think about it to this day. I partake of the sacrament much differently since then. I often think of that time and what a blessing it is to be worthy to partake of the sacrament each time the opportunity arrives. I also remember the day I was told that my friend had been re-baptized. With deep reverence for the Atonement, I thought how much I would have liked to have been present with him that first Sunday when he was able to partake of the sacrament again. I would have loved to have been there with him as he partook and then passed the sacrament tray to me. Though I wasn't there in person, I was in thought—grateful thought."

Some may wonder at times if they are worthy to take the sacrament, even though they are eligible. Elder John H. Groberg clarified this when he said, "If we desire to improve (which is to repent) and are not under priesthood restriction, then, in my opinion, we are worthy. If, however, we have no desire to improve, if we have no intention of following the guidance of the Spirit, we must ask: Are we worthy to partake, or are we making a mockery of the very purpose of the sacrament, which is to act as a catalyst for personal repentance and improvement? If we remember the Savior and all he has done and will do for us, we will improve our actions and thus come closer to him, which keeps us on the road to eternal life" ("The Beauty and Importance of the Sacrament," *Ensign,* May 1989, 38).

I think Satan would like us to believe we're not worthy. Maybe we've lost patience with a child and behaved in ways we aren't proud of, or had a less than admirable experience with a neighbor, or any one of other numerous shortcomings. Satan would want us to magnify those experiences out of proportion and make ourselves feel unworthy. He knows the blessing that partaking of the sacrament can be in our lives, and he doesn't want that for us. On the other hand, that's exactly what the Lord wants. He wants to bless us. His whole purpose is to bring us peace, joy, and hope. It then becomes our duty and blessing to put our minds in order, desire to improve, plead for forgiveness, and savor the sweet partaking of these sacred emblems.

Extraordinary Moments

MOST OFTEN OUR EXPERIENCES DURING the sacrament service are simple and quite ordinary. We often attend meetings and don't experience anything at all extraordinary, but we still attend. Then one day, as if out of the blue, something extraordinary happens. We have an unexpected deeply spiritual experience, one that never would have happened had regular attendance not put us in the place where the extraordinary could happen.

My friend Jana Parkin shared a tender and extraordinary sacrament experience on her blog:

> Our sixteen-year-old son blessed the sacrament for the first time today. Just a few minutes earlier, a young couple gave their newborn daughter a name and a blessing. Suddenly I was reminded of a day, more than seven years ago, that

was poignant and pivotal for me. I hadn't thought about this experience for literally years. But somehow the sweetness of seeing our son up there blessing the sacrament, willingly and worthily, along with the sweetness and joy of this couple presenting their baby girl both to the ward and the Lord, culminated in a rich flashback experience that I felt compelled to write.

Seven and a half years ago we had a baby that was stillborn. The following Sunday I was well enough to go to church, but wasn't sure I was ready to greet the throngs of people there, didn't want them fussing over me and talking about the stillbirth, no matter how much I loved them all. Yet I felt this almost desperate longing to go to church and take the sacrament. So a friend helped me look up the meeting times for a ward in another area, and away I went, all by myself. I just wanted to be invisible, anonymous. I was hoping to slip in unnoticed, get lost in the sea of faces, and worship.

It wasn't a fast Sunday, but for some reason right between the opening announcements and the sacrament a young father stood up to bless his newborn baby. There it was, the very thing I was trying to escape, staring me right in the face. The depth of my sadness, coupled with the shock of seeing that baby being blessed, was so intense it felt like someone stabbed me right through the heart with a knife. I felt actual physical pain.

But then came the sacrament. As I pondered the Savior and sought His peace, the most amazing feeling swept over me. It was almost like "there could be nothing so exquisite and so bitter as were my pains. Yet, there can be nothing so exquisite and sweet as was my joy."

Comfort. Healing. Peace. Not only was my pain swept away; I felt enveloped in love.

I don't remember ever feeling as grateful for the sacrament as I did at that moment. I wish I could have that poignant and powerful an experience every week. But I know the sacrament is the most important part of our Sunday worship. I wept as I saw our son up there blessing the bread and water for the first time. And I'll always remember that amazing Sunday when I learned that no one goes unnoticed in His eyes. ("No One Goes Unnoticed In His Eyes," http://reaching4rubies.blogspot.com/)

We, Too, Can Be Filled

BY OUR CONSISTENT ATTENDANCE AND partaking of the sacrament, the Lord will use the way He has provided to heal our hearts and bring peace to our souls. We need to be where He is—where He has commanded us to be each Sunday, participating in "the grandeur of this sacred ordinance." As we do this, it may be said of us, like the Nephites of old during that first administration of the sacrament, "[they did eat and] . . . they did drink, and they were filled" (3 Ne. 18:9).

Thanks to dear friends and family members who shared their experiences with me and gave permission to use them in this chapter.

COME UNTO CHRIST AND HIS SACRAMENT

By E. Douglas Clark

The Modern Miracle of the Sacrament

FROM THE BEGINNING, THE MESSAGE trumpeted by all the prophets has been what Moroni declared in his farewell: "Come unto Christ. . . . Yea, come unto Christ" (Moro. 10:30, 32). The Savior's own invitation was recorded by the prophet Alma: "He sendeth an invitation unto all men, for the arms of mercy are extended towards them, and he saith: Repent, and I will receive you. Yea, he saith: Come unto me and ye shall partake of the fruit of the tree of life; yea, ye shall eat and drink of the bread and the waters of life freely" (Alma 5:33–34).

The promised blessings can, I believe, begin here and now. Every Sunday, Latter-day Saints throughout the world *do* come to Him in the spirit of repentance, congregating with faith in His promise that when they meet together, He will be there also (see D&C 6:32). Having already "entered in by the gate" of baptism by "relying wholly upon the merits of him who is mighty to save," they seek to "press forward, feasting upon the word of Christ" (2 Ne. 31:18–20).

And He, true to His word, *does* give them to "eat and drink of the bread and the waters of life freely." By the hands of His priesthood holders (see D&C 36:2), He reaches out and offers each of us, one by one, bread in remembrance of His body, and drink in remembrance of His blood once shed for us. By partaking of these sacred emblems, we witness our willingness to take upon ourselves His name, promising to "always remember him and keep his commandments . . . that [we] may always have His spirit to be with [us]" (D&C 20:77, 79).

This weekly ritual begins with a hymn, as did the Savior's Last Supper, and is administered usually by teenage priesthood holders who pray over the bread and water and then offer them to each member. The ordinance proceeds in silence save for the occasional prattle of little children, a gentle reminder that to come to Him we must "become as a little child" (3 Ne. 37–38).

Reverently and without ostentation, we offer our meager sacrifice of "a broken heart and a contrite spirit" (3 Ne. 9:20), while He, through the cosmic power of His atoning sacrifice, abundantly pours forth His Spirit upon us—as happened at this dispensation's first sacrament service on April 6, 1830: "the Holy Ghost was poured out upon us to a very great degree," recorded the Prophet Joseph (*History of the Church,* 1:74–78).

And so it continues today. Partaking worthily of the Savior's sacrament, we are filled with His tender and transforming mercy. Repented-for sins are forgiven; broken hearts are mended; discouraged souls are comforted; perplexed minds are enlightened; faithful Saints are strengthened; and private burdens are lifted— burdens not just of sin, but of the gamut of human pain and perplexity. To the mother grieving over a wayward child, to the father struggling to provide for his family, to the person wrestling with addiction, the Savior speaks peace and hope and guidance.

A casual observer may be oblivious to such spiritual manifestations, but for the Latter-day Saints who experience them, they are nothing short of miraculous. "The greatest miracles I see today," observed President Harold B. Lee, "are not necessarily the healing of sick bodies, but . . . the healing of sick souls" ("Stand Ye in Holy Places," *Ensign*, Jul. 1973, 122).

In this miracle of the Lord's Spirit resting mightily upon His latter-day congregations, there may be an echo of the ancient miracle of the Lord's presence protecting the camp of Israel: by day they were led by a cloud of glory, and by night a pillar of fire provided light (see Ex. 13:21–22). If that ancient marvel was more visible, our modern one seems more significant, for this is a fire that burns in our hearts, and a glory that shines in our souls (see 3 Ne. 9:20). It may well be part of what Joseph Smith prophesied: "The Spirit of God will be showered down from above, and it will dwell in our midst. The blessings of the Most High will rest upon our tabernacles" (*Teachings of the Prophet Joseph Smith*, 231).

By means of His sacrament, the Lord is extending the power of His Atonement to His Saints, progressively refining them so "that when he shall appear we shall be like him, . . . that we may be purified even as he is pure" (Moro. 7:48). This remarkable transformation is surely one of the great miracles of the Lord's "marvellous work and a wonder" (Isa. 29:14) as His people prepare for the future by always remembering Him.

Remembering Him and His Last Supper

President Spencer W. Kimball taught:

> When you look in the dictionary for the
> most important word, do you know what it
> is? It could be "remember." . . . Our greatest
> need is to remember. That is why everyone
> goes to sacrament meeting every Sabbath
> day—to take the sacrament and listen
> to the priests pray that "they may always
> remember him and keep his commandments
> which he has given them." "Remember"
> is the word. "Remember" is the program.
> ("Circles of Exaltation," address to Seminary
> and Institute Personnel, Brigham Young
> University, June 28, 1968)

The sacrament prayers teach that we are to remember
Him not only by keeping His commandments but also
by keeping Him in our thoughts. I have come to believe
that this remembering includes a uniquely personal
and private dimension. For me, remembering Him
means recalling His mercies and miracles in my own
life, His forgiveness of my sins and His patience with
my weaknesses, and the blessings and opportunities He
constantly and lovingly affords me. Remembering Him
means contemplating how different my life would be
without His boundless mercy.

Remembering Him also means remembering the
price He paid to provide that mercy. As His atoning hour
approached, He met with His Apostles in an upper room

in Jerusalem to celebrate the Passover. I wonder if the purpose was to prepare not only them but perhaps also Himself for what loomed in Gethsemane that evening and at Calvary the next day.

As their forefathers had done for many generations, Jesus and His Apostles were commemorating the miracle of the first Passover in Egypt. There the God of Israel had shielded His people as the destroying angel killed every firstborn but passed over the households whose doorposts were smeared with the blood of a sacrificial lamb (see Ex. 12).

Did the Apostles understand that among them at this Passover was the very Lamb of God, He to whom all the Passover lambs pointed? As Jesus broke the unleavened bread and gave it to them, did they understand that He was the bread of life, the true manna from heaven? (See John 6:48–51.) As He passed around the cup of wine, did they comprehend that He was the true vine? (See John 15:1.)

And did they grasp the stunning fact that He who offered this memorial meal was in fact the very God of Israel, He who had shielded their forefathers in Egypt, and He whose blood—so strikingly symbolized by the dark wine—was about to be shed for their redemption? From now on, He told them, they were to eat this meal not in remembrance of the miracle in Egypt, but of what that first Passover—and every one since—had foreshadowed: Him and His perfect Atonement, the "great and last sacrifice" (Alma 34:14). The bread would be eaten in remembrance of His body, the wine drunk in remembrance of His blood.

They were to remember also the great commandment He now gave them, which explained His own motive and the model it offered for them. "This is my commandment, That ye love one another, as I have loved you. Greater love hath no man than this, that a man lay down his life for his friends" (John 15:12–13).

When the meal was over and His final instructions were ended, Jesus left to make what Elder Jeffrey R. Holland called the "loneliest journey ever made," namely, the thing that He alone could do—to pay the price for our sins ("None Were with Him," *Ensign,* May 2009, 86). This journey took place, according to the Gospel of John, on Passover, the fifteenth day of the first month of the Jewish calendar. As Jesus hung on the cross, the Passover lambs were being slain in the temple area (see John 13:1–20; and R. E. Brown, *The Gospel According to John,* 2:555–556). In the words of the Apostle Paul, "Christ our passover is sacrificed for us" (1 Cor. 5:7).

Remembering a Nephite Passover

As Christ the Creator hung on the cross, His creations trembled in agony. The Gospel of Matthew reports that "there was darkness over all the land," and when Jesus died, "the veil of the temple was rent in twain from the top to the bottom; and the earth did quake, and the rocks rent" (Matt. 27:45, 51).

It was part of what had been foretold long ago in ancient Israel, as recorded in the Book of Mormon: "the rocks of the earth must rend; and because of the groanings of the earth, many of the kings of the isles of the sea shall be wrought upon by the spirit of God, to exclaim: The God of nature suffers" (1 Ne. 19:12). The book also describes a cataclysmic storm—"such an one as never had been known in all the land"—that rocked the New World while Jesus hung on the cross. Never had there been such terrible lightning, thunder, whirlwinds, and earthquakes, which for three hours wreaked geologic havoc and widespread human destruction. Entire cities were burned or buried alive or swept into the sea, followed by a "thick darkness" penetrated only by the "great and terrible" howling of the survivors (see 3 Ne. 8:5–25).

Then came a voice, the voice of the Son of God, who had just finished His Atonement and entered the spirit world. Those who had perished, He explained, had done so "because of their wickedness and their abominations" (3 Ne. 9:12). He now invited the survivors to return and repent, repeatedly urging them to come unto Him (see 3 Ne. 9:12–14, 22).

The account gives the exact date of the storm: the fourth day of the first month, or eleven days before their anticipated Passover celebration. Such was the discrepancy that had arisen over the centuries between the Nephite calendar and the Jewish calendar, in which Jesus was crucified on Passover. In a very real sense, however, Passover arrived early for the Nephites. Only those who had, by greater righteousness than their colleagues, "appl[ied] the atoning blood of Christ" (Mosiah 4:2) were passed over in the great destruction.

Remembering His Visit to the Nephites

Some time later, as a large group of the faithful gathered at the Nephite temple, the Savior descended in broad daylight and stood before them. Extending His pierced hands, He identified Himself: "Behold, I am

Jesus Christ, whom the prophets testified shall come into the world. And behold, I am the light and the life of the world." He then spoke of a cup: "I have drunk out of that bitter cup which the Father hath given me, and have glorified the Father in taking upon me the sins of the world" (3 Ne. 11:10–11).

Having already addressed these people in the darkness after the storm, and having repeatedly invited them to come unto Him, He now repeated the invitation, made more meaningful by His personal presence:

> Arise and come forth unto me, that ye may thrust your hands into my side, and also that ye may feel the prints of the nails in my hands and in my feet, that ye may know that I am the God of Israel, and the God of the whole earth, and have been slain for the sins of the world. (3 Ne. 11:14)

The account is very specific as to what happened next.

> And it came to pass that the multitude went forth, and thrust their hands into his side, and did feel the prints of the nails in his hands and in his feet; and this they did do, going forth one by one until they had all gone forth, and did see with their eyes and did feel with their hands, and did know of a surety and did bear record, that it was he, of whom it was written by the prophets, that should come.

> And when they had all gone forth and
> had witnessed for themselves, they did cry
> out with one accord, saying:
>
> Hosanna! Blessed be the name of the
> Most High God! And they did fall down at
> the feet of Jesus, and did worship him. (3
> Ne. 11:15–17)

Only later are we told how many were in the crowd that day: 2,500! For each one to walk up to Him and gaze into His loving eyes and reverently feel His wounds would have taken hours. Why did He have them come up individually? It seems to me that it was not only out of His great love, but also to encourage each one to make the spiritual journey to Him that is required for salvation—a journey of the heart and mind, a journey of humility and repentance and resolve.

He repeatedly spoke of this spiritual journey as He proceeded to teach them. To His twelve disciples, He emphasized that they must repent and be baptized and become as a little child in order to enter the kingdom of God (see 3 Ne. 11:37–38). To the multitude, He promised that all who hungered and thirsted after righteousness would be "filled with the Holy Ghost." His whole purpose in coming to them, He said, was so that they would repent of their sins "and come unto me with a broken heart and a contrite spirit" (3 Ne. 12:6, 19).

After lengthy instruction that day, the Master Teacher saw that His students were weak and not able to understand all that He was saying. He urged them to go home and reflect on what He had said, and He would return the next day. The crowd was silent and in tears as they looked "steadfastly upon him as if they would ask him to tarry a little longer with them" (3 Ne. 17:5). Compassion filled Him, and He invited them to bring to Him all who were ill or handicapped—deaf, blind, lame, leprous, or "afflicted in any manner"—and He would heal them (3 Ne. 17:9).

Some of the afflicted were probably already in the crowd, but others—like the lepers—probably were not. His compassion reached out to those who were not there, and reached out personally; He easily could have healed them all merely by speaking the word, *without* them actually coming up to Him, as He had done at times in His mortal ministry (see Matt. 8:5–13; 15:21–28; John 4:46–54). But He insisted on taking the time to interact with each of the afflicted personally and "did heal them *every one as they were brought forth unto him*" (3 Ne. 17:9, emphasis added). Once again, it seems to me not only an act of great compassion but also an opportunity for each to come to Him spiritually. He wanted to heal not only their bodies but also their souls.

Perhaps He also wanted to teach all present that He had the power to heal them spiritually. During His mortal ministry, as another crowd had watched, He had told a crippled man that his sins were forgiven. The unbelieving onlookers were aghast. Jesus, knowing their thoughts, said, "Which is easier, to say, 'Your sins are forgiven,' or to say, 'Stand up and walk'? But so that you may know that the Son of Man has authority on earth to forgive sins. . . ." Jesus then addressed the crippled man: "Stand up, take your bed and go to your home." The man did so, and the crowd learned that this Physician had power to heal not just the body, but the soul (Matt. 9:5–8, *New Revised Standard Version*).

The Nephites standing before Him were not unbelievers, but watching Jesus heal their afflicted left no doubt that He could also heal their souls. They knew that He was indeed the Christ, and they were so moved by His love that "as many as could come for the multitude did kiss his feet, insomuch that they did bathe his feet with their tears" (3 Ne. 17:10).

Jesus then turned His attention to the little children. They had undoubtedly already come up to Him with their parents earlier that day, and so had interacted with Him and lost any fear they might have had of a stranger. Now He asked the parents to bring forth their little ones again. Surrounded by the children, He commanded the multitude to kneel. He Himself then knelt and prayed for them in words "so great and marvelous" that "no tongue can speak, neither can . . . be written." Those present later reported that "no one can conceive of the joy which filled our souls at the time we heard him pray for us" (3 Ne. 17:16, 17).

Filled with joy Himself, Jesus "wept, and . . . he took their little children, *one by one,* and blessed them, and prayed unto the Father for them." Weeping again, Jesus said, "Behold your little ones," while angels descended in glory and ministered to the children (3 Ne. 17:21–24, emphasis added). Everyone in the crowd that day had been privileged to personally interact with Jesus, but only the children received individual blessings and the ministering of angels. It was the ultimate lesson in becoming as a little child.

For the Nephites in attendance that day, it had been the greatest spiritual feast of their lives. Even so, the day had been long and they were hungry. They would soon be headed home and could eat there, but Jesus insisted on providing a meal.

At His command, the disciples brought bread and wine. He broke the bread and blessed it, whereupon each person—each who that day had come to Him and felt His tangible body—now received from Him, either from His own hand or the hand of one of His disciples, a piece of the tangible bread. Each ate and was "filled." He who had once drunk out of the bitter atoning cup then passed the cup of sweet wine, and each person—each who that day had felt the wounds from which He once bled—now drank and was "filled" (see 3 Ne. 18:1–9)—filled, we might suppose, both physically and spiritually.

This meal, He instructed, they were commanded "always" to have among those who were baptized, eating the bread "in remembrance of my body," and drinking the wine "in remembrance of my blood" (3 Ne. 18:7–11). He further explained, "I have commanded that none of you should go away, but rather have commanded that ye should come unto me, that ye might feel and see" (3 Ne. 18:25). That day they had indeed felt and seen—not only His body but also the sacred, tangible emblems thereof. And in partaking of them, they had also felt the healing power of His Spirit testifying that He was the Christ, the very Son of God.

Our Sacrament and Looking Ahead

BESIDES THE TIMELESS TRUTHS TAUGHT by the Nephite record about the sacrament, the events described actually foreshadow our day, as President Ezra Taft

Benson explained. Referring to "the record of the Nephite history just prior to the Savior's visit," President Benson emphasized "its great value for our time and our generation," including its "many parallels to our own day as we anticipate the Savior's second coming" (*A Witness and a Warning* [Salt Lake City: Deseret Book Company, 1988], 37).

As happened with the Nephites, our world will soon undergo a terrible destruction, a veritable Passover for which the Lord's people prepare each week by partaking of sacred emblems in remembrance of His body and blood. To those who keep their sacramental promises, He promises to "drink of the fruit of the vine with you on the earth" (D&C 27:5) at the great "marriage supper of the Lamb" (Rev. 19:9; see also Matt. 8:11). To them will He give access "to the tree of life" and "the water of life freely" (Rev. 22:14, 17).

Meanwhile, supping with the Savior in His sacramental meal is one of life's sublimest experiences. As we come to Him with our sacrifice of a broken heart and a contrite spirit, with an unswerving resolve to always remember Him and keep His commandments, He tenderly blesses us "one by one," healing our hearts, lifting our burdens, and filling us with unspeakable joy.

BROKEN BREAD AND MANGO
By Toni Sorenson

THE METAL FOLDING CHAIR WOBBLED. That was nothing new. Every milk-chocolate brown chair in every LDS meetinghouse I'd ever attended wobbled.

I sat as quietly as I could, trying to balance, watching people file in through double doors that swung wide to let in the steaming Caribbean air. One rail-thin man with cotton for hair hobbled in, leaning on a wooden crutch. A cluster of people rushed to aid him. A little girl in ruffles the same shade as sunshine danced in, her arm nestled in a sling. Her open-mouthed smile made my own lips curve upward in spite of the pain that surged through my body. The previous day I'd fractured my leg and six other bones, and since I was in Haiti, the Lord was giving me a poignant opportunity to empathize with the people who had survived one of the most devastating earthquakes in the world's recorded history.

I was broken.

They were broken.

The Holy Spirit kept whispering that word over and over in my mind: *broken.*

I thought I understood why. Just outside the door of our chapel lay a nation truly broken. The homes and businesses that weren't in complete rubble were fractured and unsafe to enter. The streets, lined with chunks of broken concrete and trash, were filled with people so divested they wandered aimlessly. Most of them had lost loved ones; all of them had lost their way. They could not go home, and I wondered how they could go on.

Broken.

I *thought* I understood what the Holy Ghost was trying to teach me, but I was wrong. I should have known that the Lord never dwells on the negative. The only reason He wanted me to understand the word *broken*—a word the dictionary defines as "something that is forcibly separated into two or more pieces"—is because He wanted to lead me to the hope that whatever it is that is broken, when laid before the Lord, will be made whole again.

So as I sat in unspeakable physical pain, I was allowed to witness a miracle. It wasn't a holy vision, yet it was sacred and new to my eyes. Through those open doors a line of young men walked in, all wearing freshly pressed white shirts and smiles as wide as the island of Hispaniola. With a reverence that was worthy of the temple, those young men gathered to prepare and administer the *sakreman*—sacrament.

First of all, I had no idea where they got clean white shirts, pressed like they'd just been pulled from dry cleaner's plastic. That was a marvel to me. Second, I didn't know where they obtained the huge loaves of bread, dry as Styrofoam, so when they divided the bread it broke off in dusty chunks.

It was all part of the lesson the Lord was teaching me.

I later learned that those young men refer to their white shirts as "wearing the priesthood" and would never think to come to the Lord's table attired in anything less than their very best—even if that meant they had to pool their meager resources to find clean water to wash their frayed shirts, and even if it meant they had to iron them by heating a metal iron with an actual flame. The lucky ones used electricity from the meetinghouse generator to heat an iron, but none of them would think to come unkempt in any manner.

Second, in an environment where the scant piece of broken bread might be the only morsel of food they would have to put in their mouths all day, the bread was truly sustaining . . . in both body and spirit.

I watched as they prepared the table, as they prepared the trays, as they prepared themselves. I'd participated in this holy ordinance hundreds of times in some of the darkest corners of the world, but there was something unique about this particular ordinance at this particular time and place.

There was no organ, no piano, but the spirit of reverence was there.

That morning my participation in the sacrament was anything but rote.

Truly, these people were laying down broken hearts and contrite spirits as they prepared to pick up the Lord's sacred supper.

My eyes stayed fixed as those young priesthood holders prepared the sacrament by *breaking* the bread. There was symbolism in that very act I'd never appreciated before. We take a broken piece of bread in remembrance of Christ's sacrifice, so that all that is broken within us might be made whole through Him.

As I put that droughty offering of bread into my mouth, the Spirit whispered to me that the Savior of mankind suffered and atoned for all of us, that we might not *remain* broken, but that we would be made whole through faith in Him and obedience to His commandments.

God, the Eternal Father

By partaking of the sacrament I was coming before my Maker, my Father, the One who knows and loves me best. In that moment I looked around at all of those Haitian faces, and I knew without doubt that we share the very same Father God.

we ask thee in the name of thy Son, Jesus Christ . . .

Jesus is our brother, which makes all of us family—and the only way we can make it back home to Father is through Jesus Christ.

to bless and sanctify this bread to the souls of all those who partake of it . . .

Our Father and Our Savior want *all* of us to be worthy to partake of the gospel, whether we live in Europe, America, Haiti, or Timbuktu.

that they may eat in remembrance of the body of thy Son . . .

The body of Christ is a physical symbol of our Father's design—our design. The fact that Christ would sacrifice His final breath on our behalf became so real to me that I could taste it in the texture of the bread. How could we ever forget the price that has been paid that we might be made whole again?

and witness unto thee, O God, the Eternal Fathe

How do we witness unto the Father? By the ... we live. By the way we treat one another. I looked up at the bishop, a young Haitian man whose eyes brimmed with tears as he looked out on his flock. His love and concern was unmistakable. That's how we do it—we allow our hearts, our hands, our feet, our words, and our resources to witness unto the Father that we love Him by loving each other.

that they are willing to take upon them the name of thy Son ...

When we carry the name of Jesus on our shoulders, we carry a weight that is both heavy and light. It is heavy because there is no greater responsibility in the world than to be a valiant Christian—and it is light because when we do that, Christ lifts our burden for us.

and always remember him ...

President Spencer W. Kimball suggested that the most important word in the dictionary is *remember* ("Circles of Exaltation," Address to Seminary and Institute Personnel, Brigham Young University, June 28, 1968). How do we remember Christ? We learn of Him. We try to emulate Him. And we do not allow ourselves to forget all that He has done for us. An interesting exercise is to keep a "Jesus Journal" of all the good things He does in your life. Count your blessings and, as you do, make a record. Give Him the credit and glory.

As I sat there praying, memory after memory came to me of how the Lord's hand has reached down to lift me, to touch me, and to heal my brokenness. I was orphaned as a child. He healed me. I was betrayed as a wife. He healed me. I came to Him a filthy sinner. He sent me away cleansed. I came to Him with empty hands outstretched, and I went away with more blessings than I could carry.

We remember Him best when we share what He has given us, when our healing helps to heal another that Christ places in our path. If you have been healed, remember that. Share God's goodness with another wounded soul, and lead them along the path that leads to Christ.

and keep his commandments which he has given them . . .

The scriptures state it as simply as it can be: "If ye love me, keep my commandments" (John 14:15). Because we are human, we sin. Because God is God, He can forgive our sins when we repent. We can and must reach for the sacrament with clean hands and a pure heart.

that they may always have his Spirit to be with them.

I looked around at the Haitian people. I had eaten with them, slept with them, walked and talked and learned with them. I thought I could glimpse the depth of their brokenness, and I knew this: no amount of money or technology, no amount of hope or work, could ever restore this people without the Spirit of God to comfort and direct them.

The meeting went on, and as I wet my lips, I realized that the blood of our Savior did atone for our sins, our sorrows, and our sufferings. I looked over at a faithful Haitian father who was surrounded by three young sons who were pushing against him, leaning on him, and vying for his attention. On his lap sat a toddler who had been at home with his mother when the earthquake violently shook Haiti for approximately thirty-five seconds. In that time the roof of his home collapsed, crushing his mother to death.

I saw that widowed father press his lips to the bulging wound that curved around that baby's head. I saw that father bow his head in a prayer I could only imagine. I saw tears dribble down his cheeks and splash down on that baby's outstretched hand.

Broken.

How can we ever be made whole if we are not broken?

Why would God sacrifice Jesus Christ if we did not need a Savior?

Those questions orbited my head as I hobbled around Haiti. With a makeshift boot on, the Lord blessed me to be able to perform the duties I'd come to accomplish. In the streets and in the roadside medical clinics, I witnessed devastation that no words can describe. I also witnessed resiliency that defies description.

Too, there was anger and violence that was terrifying.

Too, there was peace and song and laughter in the still-smoldering rubble.

Everywhere I went and everything I experienced brought me back to the covenant I'd made when I reached for the sacred bread and water.

Broken. I prayed to understand what the Lord wanted me to learn.

Cradling a little orphaned girl in my arms, I asked the Lord why a broken heart has to hurt *so* much.

Trying to comfort a confused man who had not been able to find his wife for weeks, I asked the Lord why suffering has to run so deep.

Abandoning my heart to a ten-year-old "misplaced" boy, I asked the Lord why so many of us lose our way.

"Kouman ou rele?" I asked the boy.

"M rele Jean Marc."

How could I make Jean Marc understand who he really was—and is? How can I make him understand that he has a Heavenly Father who loves him, that all he has to do is reach out and God will reach down?

The only answer my heart felt was a throbbing assurance that the Lord knows each of His children and loves us all in spite of whatever we've done or haven't done.

One night while I was lying on my sisal mat in the heat of the night with an onslaught of mosquitoes swarming around me, I opened my eyes to find myself nose-to-nose with a little girl's face.

"Sirèt."

I didn't have any candy, but I patted the space next to me and she rushed in to nestle next to me. In fifteen minutes there were fifty children all around me, from crawling babies to eighteen-year-old young men and women, navigating around my broken leg and ribs. Jean Marc cautioned the younger ones to be gentle with the *"blan."*

The children tried to teach me Creole, and we laughed ourselves to tears at my pronunciation.

They sang to me.

We laughed breathlessly as I sang to them.

More tears came as they broke into a song with words I did not recognize and yet I knew. The tune bore witness to my soul that everything the Lord had been teaching me was truer than true. "I Am a Child of God" in Haitian Creole is one of the most beautiful sounds you'll ever hear, especially when sung by dozens of *broken* children. The strain still echoes in my heart as I write the words you're now reading.

I knew in that instant, in that atmosphere of music, that the hope for those children, for all of us, lies in the symbolism and power of the sacrament. For we are mortals, and as mortals, we are susceptible—even prone—to injury and decay.

In other words, we all break.

Our bones break.

Our hearts break.

Our lives break.

It doesn't matter if we injure ourselves by choice or if we are injured by another; the pain is real and only One can heal us no matter how or where we're broken.

I testify to you that Jesus is that One.

Over the course of my time in Haiti, Jean Marc and I became very close. He did not know his father. He had no siblings. In the earthquake he had been separated from his mother. I ached to take him home and make him my family, but that was not possible.

I did not call him Jean Marc. I called him *Mango* because every morning, without fail, that barefooted little boy would shimmy up what I took to be the tallest tree in all of Haiti just to bring me a fresh mango for my breakfast. He didn't want to share. He wanted me to have it all, and delighted at my silly attempts to peel and eat it correctly. I always came away with mango pulp strung between my teeth and yellow juice dripping down my chin. He would howl at me and say the only three English words he knew: "God bless you."

On the day I returned to America, Mango departed on a trip of his own. Word had come that his mother was some fifty miles away, on the opposite side of the river. He set out to find her.

I panicked and tried to make safe travel arrangements for him.

I wanted to take him there myself.

I wanted to make sure he was safe.

All my wants only interfered with his plans and the way such things are done in Haiti. You see, it's not at all unusual for a child of ten or even younger to wander the country alone.

You can imagine my motherly angst as Mango and I parted. All I had to offer were a few American dollars and a tube of antibacterial ointment in case he scraped himself along the way.

"God bless you," he said to me, offering one last mango.

I hugged him so tight mango juice dripped onto his bare toes and onto my makeshift cast.

When I came back to America, I attended another, very different LDS meeting. When I sat on another wobbly chocolate-brown metal chair, I thought about the lessons I'd learned in Haiti as the sacrament was administered.

First, we are all children of a God who knows us and loves us.

Second, we have a Savior because we need saving. But we have to reach out to Christ, who stands ready and reaching to save us. Why do you think we "take" the sacrament? I believe it's symbolic—He offers, but we have to reach and "take" what He offers. We have to do our part for the covenant to function as a two-way promise.

Third, I have *repented* of sending my boys to church in wrinkled white shirts, hoping their ties are wide enough to camouflage my lack of ironing. I have also repented of more significant sins because I do not want to ever reach for that broken bread or cup of holy water with unclean hands.

Fourth, I try to *remember* all the good things that have come my way through mercy and grace. *Remembering* is the key to gratitude.

Fifth, I want to take His name upon me and to have His Spirit to be with me, so I try a little harder to love a little better. I think of how Jesus showed love the first time He administered bread and wine to His chosen Twelve—even to Judas, knowing and loving Judas better than Judas knew and loved himself.

Sixth, I see those broken pieces of bread with all their jagged edges, and I think of the pain and suffering in my own life and in the lives of so many others. How could such brokenness ever be made whole again? And yet I know the Atonement of Jesus Christ has the power to do just that.

Because I partook of the sacrament in a broken country, surrounded by broken people, the sacrament will never again to me be just a ritual. It will forevermore be an act of worship. And who's to say that the people sitting around me in my American ward are not just as broken as the Haitians? Only God can see the heart.

As I think of Christ, an image of Mango's black face and blinding smile fills my mind and soul. My eyes brim with tears and my heart breaks right down the middle. I wonder if he is safe. I wonder if he ever found his mother. I wonder who is taking care of *my* Mango.

Slowly the crack down the center of my heart begins to knit.

The Holy Spirit whispers the balm I need.

Though I don't know where Mango is, or how he is, Heavenly Father knows. Jesus has already paid the price to feel that boy's pain, so Mango doesn't have to suffer. No matter what happens to Mango, no matter what happens to break our worlds apart or to break us into pieces, we can all be made whole again by the One who designed us in the beginning. He knows us. He loves us because we are His.

All this and so much more is found in the ordinance of the sacrament. I challenge you to repent more deeply, feel more profoundly, search with greater intensity for meaning and significance in your own lives every time you reach to "take" the blessed and sanctified bread and water. I know I need to.

As the deacons return the empty bread and water trays, as the priests cover them over in sacred white, I bow my head and say a three-word prayer that lets the Lord know I'm beginning to understand the sacrament lessons He so diligently and lovingly taught me in Haiti: "God bless Mango."

A TEENAGER LEARNS ABOUT THE SACRAMENT

By Hank Smith

It has been my great joy to work with the youth, and I love them. It is my fervent desire that these young men and women learn in their youth what it means to have the opportunity to partake of the sacrament and what it can mean in their lives. My contribution, then, differs in tone from those of the other works found between the covers of this book. That difference is not because I view the sacrament lightly, but because I have directed my words to the youth I love in language I hope resonates with them.

I'LL NEVER FORGET THAT DAY in sacrament meeting. Back then, I was a typical teen, bored and inattentive, waiting for the clock to slowly tick around to ten after the hour. And then one Sunday, while sitting on the same bench as a family I had known since childhood, I noticed that the daughter—a girl about my age—kept her cup after the sacrament had been passed. She sat listening to the speaker, popping the plastic with her teeth.

Suddenly, she drew a sharp breath to cough, and the cup had nowhere to go but straight down her windpipe. Her eyes bulged and her hands clutched at her throat. She gasped, frantic (but trying to be silent), motioning to her dad. He rushed her out of the meeting, followed by her mom and two brothers. Since I was now the only one left on the bench, I decided to see if they needed help.

I found them just outside the meetinghouse, her mom in a panic, her dad attempting a few creative variations of the Heimlich maneuver. Fortunately, the cup only partially blocked her airway, but her pained expression and labored breathing made it clear that she wasn't enjoying the experience. After a few tense moments, her father dislodged the sacrament cup and she was okay. In fact, we returned to the meeting with a few minutes to spare, acting as if nothing out of the ordinary had happened—nothing more than a quick family field trip to the front lawn. As we sat back down on the bench, I thought to myself, *This was the coolest sacrament meeting ever!*

I can see now that the only real tragedy that day was my attitude and my perception of the sacrament. How was it that I completely missed the best part of the week every Sunday? How could I sit bored and miss out on a limitless spiritual experience when it was right in front of me? Multiple times the Savior has said, "I am the light which shineth in darkness, and the darkness comprehendeth it not" (see D&C 6:21; 10:58, 34:2, 39:2; 45:7).

The Prophet Joseph Smith taught that "the Atonement of the Only Begotten Son of God in the flesh is the . . . greatest expression of divine love this world has ever been given. Its importance in the Church of Jesus Christ of Latter-day Saints cannot be overstated. Every other principle, commandment, and virtue of the restored gospel draws its significance from this pivotal event" (*Teachings of the Presidents of the Church: Joseph Smith*, 9).

If I understand the Prophet correctly, he is saying that the Atonement is the most important thing that has ever happened or ever will happen. *Ever.* And since the Atonement is "the greatest expression of divine love this world has ever been given," then it comes as no surprise that an Apostle has told us that the sacrament itself—by which we remember the Atonement—makes sacrament meeting the most important meeting in the Church (see Dallin H. Oaks, "Sacrament Meeting and the Sacrament," *Ensign,* Nov. 2008, 17–20).

My experience as a teenager is a real example of how someone can eat a piece of bread and drink a small cup of water at Church each week but never really experience the sacrament. I had no idea what I was missing. I was clueless, but you don't have to be. The sacrament can (and should) be the most sacred, important, and cool part of your week.

Isaiah and the Sacrament

Take a look with me at the vision Isaiah had as he began his ministry; an account of his experience is found both in the Bible (see Isa. 6) and in the Book of Mormon (see 2 Ne. 16).

Isaiah saw "the Lord sitting upon a throne, high and lifted up, and his train filled the temple" (Isa. 6:1). As you'll see in the footnote, this *train* is reminiscent of the train of a wedding dress—the part of the dress that trails behind or follows the bride as she walks—and likely indicates that Isaiah was in a sacred place, gathered with a lot of "followers" of Christ.

In verse 2, Isaiah tells us that among the assembly were angels with great power (the power to move and act is symbolized by the wings). These angels speak to the group, which tells us they have significant authority.

In verse 3, one of the angels speaks to the group in a very sacred manner. Notice that the angels showed great reverence by covering their faces. In addition, Isaiah uses repetition in order to emphasize a point. In this case, the word *holy* is used three times in verse 3—indicating that the angel's message is apparently extremely holy.

At the end of verse 4, the whole house is filled with smoke; smoke is often a symbol of prayer and is a symbol of the Holy Ghost in the Old Testament. In the ancient tabernacle (somewhat like a tent) that Moses and the children of Israel built after they left Egypt, the priest was to burn incense—sending smoke into the air—every morning and every evening, just as we say our morning and evening prayers today. Building on what we learned in the previous verse, it seems that the angel said a very sacred and holy prayer. Since the entire house was filled with smoke, everyone there—including Isaiah—was likely praying and feeling the Spirit.

In verse 5 Isaiah expresses that he feels "undone" and that he has "unclean lips." In our words, he would be saying, "Lord, I feel horrible about the things I've done wrong! I feel unworthy." The Lord cannot look upon sin with the least degree of allowance, and Isaiah knows it. He feels cut off and overwhelmed as he realizes how truly repulsive all sin is when compared to the glory and goodness of our Heavenly Father. As we know, the Holy Ghost was present—and it is the Holy Ghost who helps us see "things as they really are" (Jacob 4:13).

Then, in verse 6, one of the angels approaches Isaiah with something in his hand: a live coal that he picked up off the altar (a structure where animals were sacrificed in accordance with the law of Moses). To get a good idea of what was happening, think of picking up a reddish-white briquette off a hot barbecue. Since the sacrifice on the altar represents the Atonement of the Lamb of God, it is interesting to note that Isaiah uses the term *live coal.* The word *live* reminds me of a well-loved hymn: "I Know That My Redeemer Lives"(*Hymns,* No. 136). He was very much alive in Isaiah's time, and He is very much alive today.

At this point in Isaiah's vision, things take a strange turn. In verse 7, we learn that the angel comes down to Isaiah with that hot coal in his hand and puts that white-hot coal on Isaiah's lips! Remember that Isaiah felt that his lips were unclean? Well, read what the angel says next: "Thine iniquity is taken away." In other words, "Isaiah, you are forgiven of your sins." Did Isaiah's cleansing really require a burning coal? Well, to be honest, real and lasting repentance is painful. It requires that we strengthen the thing that makes us weak. It requires a broken heart and a contrite spirit.

Why is being cleansed from sin and being strengthened against future temptation worth suffering? Because we are becoming clean again and our worthiness and spiritual strength is more important to us than our comfort. Why do you put yourself through the suffering of lifting massive weights every day in the weight room? Because the change and the growth you want requires some pain. The joy of being physically fit is worth the pain of working out—and, in the same way, the joy of a changed heart is well worth the pain of repentance. When Alma the Younger reflected on the difficulty of repentance, he told his son Helaman that his "soul was filled with joy as exceeding as was [his] pain" (Alma 36:20). True repentance is always painful, but it is always followed by true joy.

Now let's put those seven verses together. Isaiah is in a sacred meeting with a lot of followers of Christ. An angel with authority says a sacred prayer. Isaiah expresses his unworthiness and his sorrow for his sins. Something is brought to him from an altar that represents the Savior's Atonement. He puts the emblem of the Savior's sacrifice to his lips, and his sins are forgiven. Does that sound familiar? It does, because it describes a sacrament meeting.

Now you can see the significance of verse 8. The Lord asks, "Whom shall I send?" and Isaiah responds, "Here am I, send me." Isaiah uses the same words the Savior used in our premortal existence when He accepted His role as the Savior in the plan of happiness (see Abr. 3:27). By using those words, Isaiah promises that he will pattern his life after the example of the Savior. In verses 8–11, just like the Savior, Isaiah accepts the mission Heavenly Father has for him.

When the Savior introduced Himself to the Nephites, one of the first things He said to them was, "I have suffered the will of the Father in all things from the beginning" (3 Ne. 11:11). What was the Father's will for the Savior? When you look up at the sacrament table on Sunday and you watch the priests carefully cover the bread and water with a white cloth, imagine the Savior's actual body lying under that cloth.

As we take the sacrament, like Isaiah, we promise to pattern our life after the Savior. That means allowing our will to be swallowed up in our Father's will (see Mosiah 15:7).

Take a minute to think about and answer these questions:

1. How could Isaiah's experience with the sacrament change my experience with the sacrament?

2. Do I see those young Aaronic Priesthood holders as angels with power and authority?

3. Do I appreciate the sacredness of the sacrament?

4. Do I see the sacrament table as an altar that holds emblems of sacrifice?

5. Am I willing to experience the pain of repentance and change?

6. Do I inwardly express my own personal commitment to pattern my life after the Savior?

The next time you partake of the sacrament, try thinking about Isaiah's repentance and commitment; if you do, you'll find your personal experience with the sacrament much more moving and inspiring. The Prophet Joseph Smith said, "God does not look on sin with allowance, but when men have sinned, there must be allowance made for them" (*Teachings of the Prophet Joseph Smith*, 240–41). That allowance can be made only because of and through the Savior. He fulfilled the penalties of justice so we wouldn't have to do so. Like Isaiah, when we partake of the sacrament, we take part in the "allowance made" for us. The cleansing power of forgiveness is what allows and motivates and inspires us to renew our resolve to pattern our lives after the Savior.

Remember Him, Not Past Sins

I DON'T KNOW ABOUT YOU, but I really hate sin. I hate how sinning makes me feel inside. Occasionally, someone will comment to me, "I wish I could be baptized again. It would be nice to feel that clean again." If you have ever felt that way, mark these lines in your own copy of *True to the Faith*: "You receive great blessings when you keep the baptismal covenant. As you renew it, the Lord renews the promised remission of your sins" (p. 148).

Isn't that wonderful! The Lord has provided the sacrament so you can feel that clean again each and every week if you keep your baptismal covenant.

In my personal study of the baptismal covenant, I've noticed that the Savior places a great deal of emphasis on our promise to remember Him. I'm not sure if you've noticed, but of the three covenants we renew as part of the sacrament prayer on the bread, only one is carried over to the sacrament prayer on the water—"that they do always remember Him."

When the Savior first instituted the sacrament in Jerusalem just before His death, Luke records: "And he took bread, and gave thanks, and brake it, and gave unto them, saying, This is my body which is given for you: this do in remembrance of me" (Luke 22:19). And when He first instituted the sacrament among the Nephites, the Savior said: "And this shall ye always observe to do, even as I have done, even as I have broken bread and blessed it and given it unto you. And this shall ye do in remembrance of my body, which I have shown unto you. And it shall be a testimony unto the Father that ye do always remember me" (3 Ne. 18:6–7).

Why is remembering the Savior so critical to our sacrament experience? I personally feel that the Savior is not only telling us what to remember, but what *not* to remember. When we have the cleansing experience of the sacrament and the Lord renews the promised remission of our sins, we seem to have a natural tendency to sabotage the experience by needlessly remembering all of our past sins.

When the Savior directs us to always remember Him, He is also directing us to not always remember our past sins. Dwelling on our previous mistakes or the mistakes of others is depressing and discouraging. Think back to the example of Isaiah. Notice that Isaiah doesn't continue to tell us about his "unclean lips" after his sacrament experience. The cleansing power of forgiveness has closed and sealed the door on his past sins. He doesn't bring them back up, and neither should we. The Anti-Nephi-Lehies didn't spend any time digging up the weapons they had buried. The Lord clearly states, "I, the Lord, will forgive whom I will forgive, but of you it is required to forgive all men" (D&C 64:10). Part of the requirement to forgive *all* men is to forgive *yourself.*

When I was a boy my mom spent a lot of time helping me correctly place Band-Aids on my knees, where it seemed I constantly had scrapes, scratches, and scabs. I often had a seemingly brand-new pair of pants with two big holes in the knees. Once the bandages came off, I just couldn't seem to leave the scabs alone. I can still hear my dad's voice hollering, "Hank, stop picking at those scabs; if you don't leave them alone, they will leave a scar." Why was it was so difficult for me to leave them alone and let them heal? We do the same thing with our *spiritual* scabs—we keep picking at old wounds that the Savior sacrificed to heal.

Listen to your Heavenly Father kindly saying, "Stop picking at that old sin—you're going to leave a scar."

If we want the healing power of forgiveness to mend and restore us from our sins and the sins of others, we have to stop picking at them. Please leave them alone and let them heal. It is no wonder the Savior is directing us to always remember Him: He wants us to stop picking at those old wounds—yet so many of us aren't taking advantage of the opportunity to be cleansed, to remember Him instead of the sins for which we have repented.

If you have a tendency to allow your yesterdays to hold your tomorrows hostage, please do yourself a favor and refuse to negotiate with terrorists! Throw out those thoughts and look forward.

You can probably guess by now that my attitude about and perception of the sacrament has changed since I was seventeen. These days, my sacrament experience isn't limited to eating a piece of bread and drinking a small cup of water at Church each week. I now recognize that the sacrament is the most sacred, important, and cool part of my week. And to help me remember, I think about the Savior—both the way He lived and the way He died—during the sacrament.

I'm no longer sitting in the dark, missing out on the spiritual light that surrounds me. I've discovered that the way I feel about the Savior and the Atonement is directly related to the way I feel about and experience the sacrament—and the same applies to you. As the Atonement becomes increasingly more important to you, the sacrament will become increasingly more important to you. The sacrament will become a light, pointing you to a bright and exciting future.

SACRAMENT OF THE LORD'S SUPPER

By Margaret McConkie Pope

THE PARTAKING OF THE SACRAMENT of the Lord's Supper is one of the most sacred ordinances of The Church of Jesus Christ of Latter-day Saints. Associated with it are principles fundamental in character-building and essential to man's advancement and exaltation in the kingdom of God. Too few attach to this simple rite the importance and significance that it merits.

Can you think of a more significant form of worship than partaking of the Lord's Supper? How many of us outwardly comply without our souls truly acknowledging its deep spiritual significance?

The Sunday before His atoning sacrifice, Jesus secured a donkey on which He rode through the gates into Jerusalem. Matthew reveals that a "very great multitude" (Matt. 21:8) of people who knew Him placed palm branches in His way. Jesus' triumphal entry into Jerusalem was in clear view of the soldiers around the temple. It seemed to warrant no Roman intervention. Strange—it took place in the immediate sight of the temple, and by Roman law, it warranted intervention. Yet there was none. Surely the soldiers were aware of the crowd that was gathering around Jesus, and at that point the decision was made to arrest Jesus in a more private situation. It became abundantly clear that Jesus would have to be taken quietly.

Many shouted, "Hosanna to the Son of David" (Matt. 21:9). The disciples made it clear, with enthusiasm, that this man was the Jewish Messiah of whom it was prophesied. He was not a pretender to the throne of King David.

The following Monday Jesus left for Jerusalem in the early morn. Disturbed to see many who bought and sold money, He overthrew the tables of the money changers, proclaiming, "My house shall be called the house of prayer; but ye have made it a den of thieves" (Matt. 21:13). Later in the day He returned to Bethany.

Tuesday Jesus entered the temple. "And when he was come into the temple, the chief priests and the elders of the people came unto him as he was teaching, and said, By what authority doest thou these things? and who gave thee this authority?" (Matt. 21:23). He answered with parables, the last time He taught in public.

On Wednesday, He rested at the home of Lazarus in Bethany. The Gospel writers are silent as to the proceedings of this day.

On Thursday, the arrangements were made to celebrate the last feast of the Passover that Jesus was to attend in His mortal life. When the meal was finished, the Savior instructed His disciples—and the sacrament of the Lord's Supper was first initiated. I invite you to join me in a consideration of the ordinances that refer to the sacrament. We will discuss these ordinances as well as one covenant.

The covenant is the new and everlasting covenant—the gospel of Jesus Christ. What makes this covenant glorious is that the Lord has promised that He will exalt all who obey these three ordinances—baptism, sacrifice, and sacrament—if they accept and have been obedient. We accept this covenant when we are baptized for a remission of our sins, for entrance into the Church, and for future admission into the kingdom of heaven. Jesus Himself broke the bread and prepared the wine.

The sacramental emblems are eaten in remembrance of the broken flesh and spilt blood of Him who died on Calvary. "Drink ye all of it; For this is in remembrance of my blood of the new testament, which is shed for as many as shall believe on my name, for the remission of their sins" (Matt. 26:27–28; JST, Matt. 26:22–24). Each of these ordinances is performed in similitude of the atoning sacrifice by which salvation comes.

How do we eat the Lord's flesh and drink His blood? Is this literal or figurative?

To eat the flesh and the blood of the Son of God is (1) to accept Him in the most literal and full sense—with no reservation—as the personal offspring in the flesh of the eternal Father and (2) to follow the Son by joining His church, keeping the commandments, and enduring to the end.

The Saints of the ancient Church were to keep the feast only in a spiritual sense. The Apostle Paul said, "Therefore let us keep the feast, not with old leaven, neither with the leaven of malice and wickedness; but with the unleavened bread of sincerity and truth" (1 Cor. 5:8).

In the partaking of the sacrament, there is the danger of permitting formality to supersede spirituality; when such is the case, the ordinance may prove to be a curse instead of a blessing. Where may our thoughts go during the sacrament? President Joseph Fielding Smith taught that during the sacrament a bishop should not be thinking about when his next meeting is and what needs to be discussed; even though those are needful thoughts, they are not what he should be thinking about during the sacrament. Likewise, a Relief Society president should not spend the sacrament wondering if all the sisters in the ward were visited that month.

"If one goes through the motion 'through meaningless' daily prayers' and 'weekly sacrament rituals' you will find yourself compromising your principles, and integrity, under the buffeting pressures of life. You will lose both the companionship of the Holy Ghost and your own self respect. You will find yourself pretending, playing the roles, focusing on clothes, tools, cars, and other material possessions all in an effort to win the approval popularity of others. But people's opinions are fickle and provide no security. When we partake of the sacrament worthily, it actually does satisfy our souls and improve our living. Also we become a witness for Christ" (Stephen R. Covey, *Spiritual Roots of Human Relations* [Salt Lake City: Deseret Book Company, 1970], 3).

We can understand partially the Savior's words:

> For behold, I, God, have suffered these
> things for all, that they might not suffer if
> they would repent;
>   But if they would not repent they must
> suffer even as I;
>   Which suffering caused myself, even
> God, the greatest of all, to tremble because
> of pain, and to bleed at every pore, and to

suffer both body and spirit—and would
that I might not drink the bitter cup, and
shrink—

Nevertheless, glory be to the Father, and
I partook and finished my preparations unto
the children of men. (D&C 19:16–19)

What is the purpose of the sacrament? We enter
into a covenant to keep the commandments, to always
remember Him. We take upon ourselves His name. We
renew the covenants we made at baptism.

Who should partake of the sacrament? Members of
the Church should partake of the sacrament, because
they are the ones who covenanted at baptism to keep His
commandments.

Where does worthiness enter into the picture?

The scriptures provide the answer (see 3 Ne. 18:28–
29; 1 Cor. 11:23–30). Personal worthiness is what
qualifies us to receive the blessings and ordinances of
the gospel. Every ordinance must be ratified by the
Holy Ghost, meaning the Holy Spirit of Promise. If you
have questions, see your bishop. We bind the Lord by
keeping His commandments: "I, the Lord, am bound
when ye do what I say; but when ye do not what I say,
ye have no promise" (D&C 82:10). Every ordinance has
a blessing and curse; those who partake of the sacrament
unworthily eat and drink damnation to their souls (see 3
Ne. 18:28–29).

Finally, sacrifice also plays a part. Elder F. Enzio Busche
said, "When we are on a spiritual plateau it is necessary
for us to understand that we cannot go beyond that
plateau until we increase our level of sacrifices and our

ability to move one step further" (*Yearning For the Living God* [Salt Lake City: Deseret Book Company, 2004], 92).

The Prophet Joseph Smith taught that "a religion that does not require the sacrifice of all things never has power sufficient to produce the faith necessary unto life and salvation" (*Lectures on Faith,* 69). The ultimate sacrifice, of course, was the Savior's; the ransom He paid delivers all of us from both temporal and spiritual death.

When we partake of the sacrament, we eat and drink in remembrance of the Pascal hour, of Gethsemane, of Calvary, and of an open tomb. The sacrament—which must be administered by legal administrators only to those who believe and have been baptized (see 3 Ne. 18:5)—is a perpetual and everlasting ordinance.

Our part is clear. By partaking, we testify to the Father that we will always remember His Son (see D&C 20:77). We renew our covenant to be the Lord's peculiar people, to set ourselves apart from the world, and to live as Saints. We make a solemn promise to keep all of the commandments (see 3 Ne. 18:10).

And what is His part? We receive glorious promises in return. As we partake worthily, we receive the promise that we will always have His Spirit to be with us (see 3 Ne. 18:11; Moroni 4; D&C 20:77). And the solid promise is there: if worthy, we will gain a remission of our sins (see JST, Matt. 26:24).

Beyond the spoken promises delivered as part of the sacramental prayer, we receive tremendous blessings. We sense a closer relationship with the Lord. We receive a feeling of peace. We recognize the opportunity to commune with the Lord and sense His nearness. We rid our hearts of ill will and hard feelings.

But the magnificent blessings of the sacrament extend beyond the promises to us as individuals. Worthy partaking of the sacrament brings to us as a people unity, love, and the power to keep God's commandments. It strengthens us as Saints. And with that simple ordinance in all its never-ending import, we are promised that thing we desire above all else: eternal life.

HUNGERING AND THIRSTING AFTER RIGHTEOUSNESS:

THE SACRAMENT AS SPIRITUAL SUSTENANCE

By Brent L. Top

HAVE YOU EVER BEEN SO hungry you thought you were going to die? I am not talking about the comparatively insignificant hunger you feel on fast Sunday when you get a little headache or your empty stomach "growls," and you *think* you're in the latter stages of starvation. I am talking about a hunger that leaves you sick and weak—drained of all strength to eat, to interact with others, or to even hold your head up. Have you ever been so thirsty that all you can think about is getting even just a few drops of water in your mouth—so thirsty that your throat feels like cotton, your muscles cramp, and your head is spinning? Have you ever been so tired that you could not bear the thought of having to expend any more energy for anything—so fatigued that you cannot sit or stand or walk? While all of us have experienced hunger, thirst, and fatigue—all part of the normal conditions of mortality—very few of us have ever experienced them to the extreme. We have, however, experienced enough to understand.

The Lord explained to the Prophet Joseph Smith that "that which is temporal [is] in the likeness of that which is spiritual" (D&C 77:2). Although given in a different context, I believe this revelation teaches us that there are spiritual counterparts to many of the things we experience in mortality. I have come to understand, both from my own personal experiences and by observing others, that spiritual hunger, thirst, and fatigue are just as real as anything physical. In fact, those spiritual deprivations usually have more damaging side-effects and life-threatening consequences than do physical deprivations—not just to that individual, but to others in their lives.

I know, too, that the sacrament of the Lord's Supper—my own covenants combined with God's promises—is a most significant remedy for spiritual hunger and fatigue. It provides the spiritual sustenance—the "filling" with the Spirit—promised those who "hunger and thirst after righteousness" (3 Ne. 12:6).

Bread from Heaven and Living Water

SHORTLY AFTER THE SAVIOR MIRACULOUSLY fed five thousand with two loaves and five fishes, He taught the people in the synagogue at Capernaum concerning miracles and manna, bread and water, and everlasting life:

> Then Jesus said unto them, Verily, verily, I say unto you, Moses gave you not that bread from heaven; but my Father giveth you the true bread from heaven.
>
> For the bread of God is he which cometh down from heaven, and giveth life unto the world.
>
> Then said they unto him, Lord, evermore give us this bread.

> And Jesus said unto them, I am the
> bread of life: he that cometh to me shall
> never hunger; and he that believeth on me
> shall never thirst. (John 6:32-35)

How is it possible to never hunger? What makes it so that one will never thirst? Not long before Jesus delivered this "Bread of Life" discourse, He told the Samaritan woman who dipped her bucket in Jacob's well: "Whosoever drinketh of this water [the water from the well] shall thirst again; But whosoever drinketh of the water I shall give him shall never thirst; but the water that I shall give him shall be in him a well of water springing up into everlasting life" (John 4:13–14). Jesus clearly teaches that it is He—not bread nor water—that will eternally satisfy hunger and quench thirst. It is His atoning sacrifice, not merely the symbols of it, that gives sustenance to our souls. More than just partaking of the bread and water, we must "partake" of the Atonement—ingest it completely, make it part of our very lives.

Consider these words of the Savior:

> I am the living bread which came down
> from heaven: if any man eat of this bread,
> he shall live forever: and the bread that I
> will give is my flesh, which I will give for
> the life of the world.
>
> The Jews therefore strove among
> themselves, saying, How can this man give
> us his flesh to eat?
>
> Then said Jesus unto them, Verily,
> verily, I say unto you, Except ye eat the

flesh of the Son of man, and drink his blood, ye have no life in you.

Whoso eateth my flesh, and drinketh my blood, hath eternal life; and I will raise him up in the resurrection of the just at the last day.

For my flesh is meat indeed, and my blood is drink indeed.

He that eateth my flesh, and drinketh my blood, dwelleth in me, and I in him.

As the living Father hath sent me, and I live by the Father: so he that eateth me, even he shall live by me. (JST, John 6:51–57)

This is one of my favorite passages in the New Testament. I love the symbolism and depth of it. It seems to jump off the page at me, rich in doctrinal significance and personal relevance.

Alive in Christ

THIS SCRIPTURE ADMONISHES US, "EXCEPT ye eat the flesh of the Son of man, and drink his blood, ye have no life in you" (John 6:53). Unless we regularly and worthily partake of the sacrament, we have, as the Savior said, no life in us. We may be alive, but not "alive in Christ" (2 Ne. 25:25). We may have life, physiologically speaking, but we will lack the abundant life He has promised (see John 10:10).

The Atonement of Jesus Christ, as symbolized by the sacramental bread and water, gives us light and life—in fact, the scriptures use the term "light of life" (John 8:12). In an eternal sense, all will be given everlasting life through resurrection to a kingdom of glory. And as resurrected beings, all will possess light and glory in a very literal sense. The Savior's promises, however, are not just reserved in waiting for some far-off day in a far-off realm. They are available right here and right now. As we covenant with the Lord through baptism, confirmation, the sacrament, and other ordinances, we commit to live our lives in harmony with His gospel. He covenants with us to fill our lives with spiritual light and abundant life.

There are two specific promises resulting from the Atonement contained in that sacramental covenant: (1) forgiveness of sins and (2) the companionship of the Holy Ghost. In these are found light and life as we sojourn in mortality

Forgiveness of Sins. Sin always brings darkness—a very real darkness that can be seen in one's countenance. In such spiritual darkness, one feels lonely, ashamed, abandoned, empty. Sometimes sin makes us feel that our life is meaningless, not worth living. Satan would have us believe that there is no hope, no light, no life—no "meaning in the madness" of mortality. Yet, the Master promises a "mighty change"—a newness of life that can lift hearts, lighten burdens, engender hope, and empower lives with greater strength to resist evil and "to do good continually" (Mosiah 5:2).

In the sacrament there is the promise of a remission of sins—a promise of a new kind of life—a life that only Christ can give to us. It is more than a "new lease on life"; it is a life in the Savior's light, a life empowered by His grace, a life enriched by His love. Without this spiritual life in Christ, promised in the sacred emblems of His sacrifice, we are as C. S. Lewis described: merely lifeless statues, made with the elements of the earth but lacking real life. When we receive a remission of sins, are born again, and become new creatures in Christ, as promised in the renewing of our baptismal covenants, we experience "as big a change as a statue which changed from being a carved stone to being a real man" (C. S. Lewis, *Mere Christianity* [New York: Macmillan, 1952], 140).

Elder John H. Groberg explained that by partaking of the sacrament worthily, we can recapture the feeling of being washed clean that we experienced at baptism (see "The Beauty and Importance of the Sacrament," *Ensign*, May 1989, 38). I have experienced that in my own life and I have seen it happen many times in the lives of others. While serving as a bishop, I gained a greater appreciation for the power of the sacrament. One experience stands out.

I received a call late one Saturday evening from a ward member. "Bishop, my wife really needs to talk to you," the husband said. We made arrangements to meet at the bishop's office first thing in the morning. The next day the husband and wife arrived at the meetinghouse hand in hand, but with eyes swollen and red from a night of crying. It seemed like an eternity before she was able to speak. When the words finally came, they flowed like a raging river that had just burst a dam.

She had carried with her the heavy burden of sin for many years. She had been promiscuous before she met her husband. He was a worthy young man and was wonderful to her. After their engagement, they prepared themselves spiritually for a temple marriage. Yet she was carrying some heavy spiritual baggage. Neither her bishop nor stake president had interviewed her thoroughly, assuming that she was worthy in every way—and she certainly appeared and acted as if she was. Immature and frightened at the time, she reasoned, *If they don't ask, I don't have to tell.* So she went to the temple unworthily. Hiding her past from her husband as well as her priesthood leaders, she continued to live a lie.

In the years since her immoral past, she had tried so hard to be as Christlike as she could be. She was one of the most pure in heart I had met. If I hadn't heard her confession with my own ears, I could never have imagined her so deeply in sin.

"I know that I will probably have to be excommunicated," she sobbed. "But I cannot carry this burden and live this lie any longer." Her heart was broken and her spirit truly contrite. She sobbed about the pain she had caused her husband when she told him of her shady past—all completely hidden from him through the years. Yet he loved her so much, and so desired her to be made spiritually whole, that it was he who had called me and had lovingly taken her by the hand to the bishop's office.

"I don't know if excommunication will be necessary," I tried to explain to her. "Before I can make any decision about what to do, I would like you to kneel with me, and let's seek the guidance of our Heavenly Father." I poured out my heart in her behalf and pleaded with God to direct me in how I could best help her find forgiveness. I asked that if it were necessary that I hold a bishop's disciplinary council for her, He would let me know. During the course of that prayer a remarkable thing happened—at least for me it was rare and remarkable. The Spirit clearly taught me, and I knew beyond a doubt what to do.

It was revealed to me that this woman had carried a tremendous burden of guilt through the years, yet had diligently tried to reform her life. The years since her marriage had been devoted to service in the Church and seeking to emulate the Savior in every way possible. The whispering of the still, small voice testified to me that her confession was now the end of her repentance process, not the beginning. There was no need for a disciplinary council—that prompting defied every ounce of logic and preconceived idea that I had before we knelt together in prayer. As I told her what I felt, the tears once again flowed freely, this time from relief and gratitude but also from the confirming witness of the Spirit. I then proceeded to give her some counsel that had clearly been given to me by the power of the Holy Ghost.

"Ordinarily I would ask you not to partake of the sacrament under these circumstances," I explained, "but the Spirit has commanded me to counsel you to partake of the sacrament today and to think deeply about what the Savior has done for you. I promise you that you will feel this burden lifted, and spiritual healing will come into your soul."

During the sacrament meeting, as we sang the sacrament hymn, I couldn't take my eyes off of her. I could see a transformation taking place. I could see renewed light and life entering her soul. There was probably more meaning in the words of the hymn to her than to the rest of the congregation. After the sacramental prayers were offered, there was the usual reverent silence as ward members pondered the Savior and His atoning sacrifice. But in that moment, her depth of remembering the Savior was unsurpassed in the chapel.

My heart was full to overflowing as I watched her partake of the bread and then bury her head in the shoulder of her husband. I could see her shoulders and body shudder as she wept. Partaking of the water, she continued to weep, but her tears were tears of joy as she smiled into the eyes of her loving and forgiving companion. I was witness to a miracle—the miracle of forgiveness, the miracle of spiritual healing, the miracle of light and life. Her countenance was changed. The brilliant light of forgiveness replaced the spiritual darkness of sin. The light was as real as rays of sunshine. In a way, her life began at that moment—a new life, an abundant life, a life in Christ.

Companionship of the Holy Ghost. Several years ago I was teaching a class of Seminary students about the covenants associated with the sacrament. "What do we promise? What does God promise?" I asked. I then wrote their responses on the chalkboard.

After I had written the responses on the chalkboard, one of the young men sitting at the back of the room blurted out, "That's not fair!"

"What do you mean by that?" I asked. "How is that not fair?"

His response caught me off guard. "Look at the lists," he said. "We promise three things and God only promises one."

I thought he was joking, but he was completely serious. He simply looked at the one promise—"that they may always have his Spirit to be with them"—

without thinking what that one promise really means. Unfortunately, many of us unwittingly do the same thing. We hear that sacramental promise every week. Perhaps it is so familiar to us that we take it for granted. What does it really mean to "always have his Spirit to be with [us]"?

I can think of no greater light to guide us in a darkened and darkening world than the Light of the World Himself. While He may not continually go before us as a pillar of fire as He did for the ancients, He has promised us something just as brilliant and illuminating—the constant companionship of the Holy Ghost. In this manner, we too can have a member of the Godhead go before us, as it were, enlightening, guiding, protecting, and comforting us.

It may be only "one gift," but its blessings to us are innumerable. The Holy Ghost is the Comforter (see John 14:16, 26). The gift of the Holy Ghost not only teaches us what we should do (see 2 Ne. 32:5) and warns us of dangers, both physical and spiritual, but also enlivens us and chases darkness from us (see D&C 93:37). It teaches us how to pray more profoundly (see 2 Ne. 32:8) and gives us greater understanding of the things of God (see 1 Cor. 12:8; Mosiah 5:3). The Holy Ghost can fill our lives with love and hope (see Moroni 8:26), peace and joy (see Gal. 5:22), and comfort in times of trial and tribulation.

The light and life—the sustaining power—that comes to us through the promise of having His Spirit always with us encompasses each of these and myriad more blessings. Elder Parley P. Pratt perhaps said it best:

> The gift of the Holy Ghost . . . quickens
> all the intellectual faculties, increases,

> enlarges, expands and purifies all the
> natural passions and affections, and adapts
> them, by the gift of wisdom, to their lawful
> use. It inspires, develops, cultivates and
> matures all the fine-toned sympathies, joys,
> tastes, kindred feelings, and affections of
> our nature. It inspires virtue, kindness,
> goodness, tenderness, gentleness, and
> charity. (*Key to the Science of Theology* [Salt
> Lake City: Deseret Book, 1979], 60–61)

Just as bread and water are sustenance for man, just as sunshine and water are needed for plants to grow, the companionship of the Holy Ghost is spiritual sustenance to the soul. As we weekly eat of the Bread of Life and drink the blood of the Lamb of God through worthily partaking of the sacrament and as we always remember Him with our whole souls, we will "not walk in darkness, but shall have the light of life" (John 8:12)—both in the eternal realms and throughout the darkness of our mortal worlds. What a great promise!

Live *By* Him

The Savior tells us, "Whoso eateth my flesh . . . even he shall live by me" (John 6:54, 57). This phrase from Jesus' Bread of Life discourse reminds me that in order for the promise of light and life—forgiveness of sins and the companionship of the Holy Ghost—to become living realities in my life, I must live *by* Him—walking with Him, striving to be more like Him. We cannot "always remember him" without also following Him. That is what you and I covenant to do when we partake of the sacrament.

There is another symbol used by the Savior in His teachings that perhaps gives us additional insight into what it means to live *by* Him. "Take my yoke upon you," Jesus commanded His disciples (Matt. 11:29). They understood that a yoke was the means whereby two oxen or donkeys could be harnessed together to work in tandem—completely unified in direction and purpose. The Apostle Paul also used the symbol of a yoke when he counseled the Saints not to be "unequally yoked" in marriage (2 Cor. 6:14).

Taking the yoke of Christ means to walk with Him as one. "Whoso eateth my flesh . . . even he shall live by me" could likewise mean, *Those who partake of the sacrament* covenant to take Christ's yoke upon themselves. We promise to live and work and love with Him, *by* Him—side by side, "equally yoked." That is no small promise—no insignificant covenant.

"Ye Shall Find Rest Unto Your Souls"

THE LORD PROMISED THOSE WHO faithfully take His yoke upon them by covenant that though they "labour and are heavy laden" they will find "rest unto [their] souls" (Matt. 11:28–29).

There is nothing more tiring than carrying the burdens of sin. There is nothing more wearying than the world and worldliness. The Savior's infinite Atonement— remembered with the sacred tokens of bread and water—can wash away wickedness and worldliness and weariness. That is the "rest" the Lord has promised. No wonder those few minutes in sacrament meeting are to be among the most sacred and profound moments of our lives. The sacrament should be, as President Gordon B. Hinckley taught, "the very heart of our Sabbath worship—a blessing without peer" (*Teachings of Gordon B. Hinckley* [Salt Lake City: Deseret Book, 1997], 561).

In my own personal life I have found that when I am struggling and weighed down—either emotionally, spiritually, or physically—the partaking of the sacrament is a source of great spiritual strength, and that those quiet, reverent moments during its administration serve as a spiritual oasis—"a refuge from the storm" (D&C 115:6). It is truly like food for the hungry, water for the thirsty, and rest for the weary. It is life-sustaining.

When I have gone for a period of time without partaking of the sacrament, I feel a very real difference in my life—something is seriously lacking. Without the sacrament I am spiritually malnourished. Perhaps you have felt that too. We are supposed to feel that way. Our spirit yearns for sustenance just as much or more than our body yearns for food and drink. And the sacrament—the "Bread from Heaven" and the "Living Waters"—provides that sustenance.

A Catalyst for Change

When I served as a bishop, I saw more clearly how the sacrament is a powerful catalyst for change in people's lives. As I counseled with ward members who had been involved in serious transgressions but were striving to fully repent, I often asked them not to partake of the sacrament "until further notice." I never put a set time for that. I knew it may require weeks, months, or even years, but I never set the time frame. I wanted it to come from them rather than from me—because I wanted them to "hunger and thirst" after the sacrament.

Too often repentance is viewed as merely the passage of time rather than the mighty change of heart that results in a transformation of attitudes and actions. When a person truly realizes what the sacrament represents— what a privilege it is to partake of it each week—and "hungers and thirsts" after the spiritual power it affords, that is a good indicator of the mighty change occurring in his or her heart and soul. In this manner, the sacrament becomes a very literal catalyst for change.

When we cannot eat of the bread or drink of the water of the Lord's Supper, we should feel a sense of loss—a spiritual hunger that has its own pains in the soul every bit as real as the physical pains of hunger experienced by one who is deprived of food. Hunger pains remind us that we need to eat. Hungering and thirsting for the sacrament similarly reminds us that we need to repent of our sins, try to be more faithful, more trusting in the Savior, and more like Him.

It shouldn't take formal Church discipline or a priesthood restriction on the partaking of the sacrament to remind us of the very real power of the sacrament. It is the means whereby God can, on a weekly basis, teach us things of the Spirit, forgive us of our sins, change our hearts, and motivate us to greater righteousness. Each of us has that privilege and promise. The sacrament can be not only a catalyst for change in our lives, but also a path of safety that reminds us on a weekly basis of our need to repent and stay true to our covenants (see Melvin J.

Ballard, "The Sacramental Covenant," *New Era*, January 1976, 9).

How thankful I am for the blessings of the sacrament. How thankful I am for the miracles I have experienced and observed in the lives of others through the sin-remitting, soul-transforming, heart-healing power that can attend that piece of bread and cup of water. May each of us more deeply "hunger and thirst" for those miracles in our own lives. May we view those moments in sacrament meeting when the emblems of our Savior's sacrifice are blessed and passed as a time of sacred reflection and solemn resolve. May our spiritual hunger be swallowed up by the Savior's love each week when His flesh and blood become part of our very souls.

A WEEKLY FUNERAL OF SANCTIFICATION

By Mary Jane Woodger

SOME WILL FIND THIS STRANGE, but I enjoy a good funeral. I don't seek out funerals, and I am not anxious for any loved one or acquaintance to die—but at times, I find in funerals something that is life-changing and reflective, something that creates a marker in my own life when another's life has ended.

I find memorial services uplifting. They remind me that the person who has left mortality is important and that a void now exists where that person once was. I find comfort from the Spirit on such occasions as one passes from mortality to immortality. When the priesthood presides at a funeral, I feel a unity among those who attend seldom found elsewhere. Menial everyday life is suspended, and discussion of the meaning of life puts things in perspective. I can now concentrate on what matters most.

At funerals, a broken heart and a contrite spirit are more easily infused into my demeanor. I find myself more reflective, with a desire to change those things in my own life that are not eulogy-worthy. The Holy Ghost fulfills His role of being a Comforter at funerals; the Spirit seems to fill the gap that is left when one leaves this frail existence.

When the eyelids of mortality have been shut for a loved one, I find more meaning in my own existence and remember that my worth stretches past the corridors of mortality. I am reminded of the worth of each life—that there is a plan, a purpose, and a meaning to entering and leaving mortality. It is with such thoughts that I am reminded that the life of all lives—the life that had the most meaning, that had the most purpose, and that was the most essential part of the plan—was the life of Jesus Christ.

Because Jesus was the most worthy of Heavenly Father's children to grace this earth, it is His life that should be the most eulogized and most remembered. It is with these thoughts that I like to approach the sacrament each Sunday. For me, the sacrament is a special memorial service, a time for me to remember the most important earthly life that makes my own life eternal.

President Spencer W. Kimball has said that the word *remember* is the most important word found in any dictionary (see "Circles of Exaltation," Address to Seminary and Institute Personnel, Brigham Young University, June 28, 1968). The scriptures constantly admonish us to remember: the word *remember* is found 220 times in the Book of Mormon alone. In all of our remembering, the most important thing for us to remember is the greatest event to have ever taken place: the Atonement of Jesus Christ. The Atonement should be our most important memory.

Remembering is the principle task of the sacrament experience. And for me, in a unique way, the sacrament is a weekly funeral. When I have approached those few sanctifying minutes in this way, letting a funeral service for the Savior drift through my mind, it has made all the difference.

Unified at the Funeral

MOST OFTEN WHEN WE ATTEND funerals we sit together as families, and the family of the deceased generally sits as a unified group. Elder Dallin H. Oaks reminds us that sacrament meeting is the only Sabbath meeting at which the entire family can attend and sit together (see "Sacrament Meeting and the Sacrament," *Ensign,* Nov. 2008, 17–20). As we attend this weekly memorial service as families or as part of a ward family, our preparation includes being unified in purpose.

We come to the sacrament with an imperfect view of ourselves and others, but we come in unity of purpose with those who surround the sacrament table.

Prayers

PRAYERS ARE SAID AT THE beginning and end of LDS funerals. Those prayers are heartfelt and specific in their wording as they invite the Spirit and prepare the participants for the funeral, a purpose slightly different from other prayers said throughout the day. So it is with the weekly sacrament service—the prayers said over the bread and water are different in purpose and content than other prayers said in LDS meetings.

President David O. McKay said of these sacrament prayers, "[The Lord] has designated a particular prayer to be offered on that occasion. He has prescribed for us only a few set prayers, one of which is the blessing on the bread and water. Now, what does it signify? You will find first that the sacrament is a memorial of Christ's life and death" (Conference Report, Oct. 1929, 10). The sacramental prayers remind us that we are to participate in memorializing our Redeemer.

The Life Sketch

During a funeral, respect is shown for the accomplishments and characteristics of the deceased as a life sketch is read. As we contemplate during the sacrament what the Savior was, is, and will be, a sort of life sketch for Him fills our minds. Elder Jeffrey R. Holland suggested some specific aspects of Christ's life that we might contemplate during the sacrament—including His premortal life, His expression of love during the grand council of heaven, His mortal birth, His miracles and teaching, and the delight He took in the opportunity to live in mortality (see "'This Do in Remembrance of Me'," *Ensign*, Nov. 1995, 67).

The life sketch given at a funeral not only includes how the person lived, but often how he or she died. The way one leaves mortality can be honored as the culmination of a life well lived, a character well developed, and a trial well endured. During the sacrament, I try to remember His bruised body and broken heart. I remember that on the cross it was the Savior's physical suffering that guaranteed, through His mercy and grace (see 2 Ne. 2:8), that every member of the human family will be freed from the bonds of death and be resurrected triumphantly from the grave. With a small, torn piece of bread, I can remember that His body was also torn by a whip made of leather strips that had shards of broken glass tied into the leather thongs.

As small drops of water sometimes drip onto my clothing from the sacrament tray or cup, I try to remember that just as grapes or olives are squeezed in a press until they give juice or oil, Christ bore an infinite weight that pressed down on Him. That weight exerted so much pressure that His skin broke at every pore. With a small cup of water I can remember the depth of His suffering as He left mortality, suffering more pain than any disease or any wound could ever inflict.

In the Garden of Gethsemane the Savior said, "My soul is exceeding sorrowful, even unto death" (Matt. 26:38). In "agony He prayed more earnestly, and his sweat was as it were great drops of blood falling down to the ground" (Luke 22:44). As I take of that small sip of water, I am reminded that among His last words were, "I thirst" (John 19:28). The soldiers gave Him gall. The last taste on His lips was bitter, but the Atonement makes the last drops of my life sweet.

Sometimes when a person suffers from a long and debilitating illness, friends and family seem to disappear as the person lingers, waiting for a welcome death. In Christ's life, family and friends also dispersed in the end. Elder Neal A. Maxwell suggested that His painful condition was the reason He asked Peter, James, and John to wait—He needed them to steady Him, to hold Him (see "In Him All Things Hold Together," *Brigham Young University Speeches of the Year,* Mar. 31, 1991). But they were exhausted and were sleeping. In His hour of greatest need, He was deserted by His closest associates.

As horrific as the Savior's tremendous physical suffering was, it was nothing compared to the spiritual and emotional anguish He encountered in the end. The

Doctrine and Covenants provides the only scriptural passage in which the Savior reveals that His suffering for sin included the Spirit's withdrawal (see D&C 19:20). President Brigham Young said of this time during Christ's Atonement that "at the very moment, at the hour when the crisis came for him to offer up his life, the Father withdrew Himself, withdrew His Spirit and cast a vail *[sic]* over him. That is what made him sweat blood; but all was withdrawn from him and a veil was cast over him, and he then plead with the Father not to forsake him" (see *Discourses of Brigham Young,* sel. John A. Widtsoe [1941], 346).

As we think of the closing hours of Christ's life, we remember His humility. In the end He did not say, "Look what I have done!" Instead, He gave glory to the Father. I often wonder how He could give the Father the glory of the Atonement. In this world of calling attention to ourselves, being aggressive, and marking our space, I can remember that the greatest sacrifice made in the universe was by One who gave someone else the credit.

In those few precious memorial moments I can remember that Jesus Christ represented the Father in the Atonement. He did for the Father what the Father could not do for Himself. As I take the water, which represents that precious blood, I try to remember that Elohim could not shed blood for mankind because He does not have any. Heavenly Father could not lay down His life because His body and sprit are inseparable. Christ did for the Father what the Father could not do, just as He did for me what I cannot do for myself. The greatest part of the life sketch of this sermon is that Jesus Christ atoned for my sins.

The Unspoken Eulogy

THE EULOGY SPOKEN AT A funeral serves both a religious and memorial purpose. It is, of course, a retelling of the admirable characteristics of the deceased, but these traits are woven into a sermon that reminds the congregation of the plan of salvation. As such, the eulogy is often a "liken unto us" part of the funeral program.

During the sacrament, I try to liken the plan of salvation in my life and the blessings of the Atonement to myself. Remembering the Atonement is not a one-time memorial service experience; the sacrament provides a weekly opportunity to remember with deep reflection—to remember in a very personal way.

In this way, the sacrament is an "unspoken eulogy," an opportunity to remember our personal weaknesses and the sins we have committed that week. It gives us a chance to commit ourselves to change. The sacrament ordinance allows us to renew our covenants and to remind ourselves where we are lacking; it is a time each week that we can remember that repentance is not easily maintained and that even a little sinning will hurt (see Dallin H. Oaks, "Sin and Suffering" *Brigham Young University Speeches of the Year,* Aug. 5, 1990). That unspoken eulogy of the sacrament also provides the opportunity to repent of our sins (see Henry B. Eyring, "That We May Be One," *Ensign,* May 1998, 66); as we recommit to doing better, the Lord renews the cleansing effect of our baptism (see Dallin H. Oaks, "The Aaronic Priesthood and the Sacrament," *Ensign,* Nov. 1998, 37).

Those few moments of contemplation during the sacrament give us the opportunity to commune with the

Lord. President David O. McKay encouraged this kind of mental concentration during the sacrament:

> You may rest assured that he will be there to inspire us if we come in proper attune to meet him. We are not prepared to meet him if we bring into that room our thoughts regarding our business affairs, and especially if we bring into the house of worship feelings of hatred toward our neighbor, or enmity and jealousy towards the Authorities of the Church. Most certainly no individual can hope to come into communion with the Father if that individual entertains any such feelings. They are so foreign to worship, and so foreign, particularly, to the partaking of the sacrament. (Conference Report, Apr. 1946, 112)

I am the first to admit that my mind wanders at times, but I have found that when I truly exert some energy to stay focused, it makes all the difference.

I like the following unspoken eulogy President Howard W. Hunter speaks of using once during the sacrament: "I asked myself this question: 'Do I place God above all other things and keep all of His commandments?' Then came reflection and resolution. To make a covenant with the Lord to always keep His commandments is a serious obligation, and to renew that covenant by partaking of the sacrament is equally serious. The solemn moments of thought while the sacrament is being served have great significance. They are moments of self-examination, introspection, self-discernment—a time to reflect and to resolve" ("Thoughts on the Sacrament," *Ensign,* May 1977, 24).

These solemn moments of thought remind us of the place that Christ has in each of our lives. A good friend inspires us to do good, and his or her eulogy may encourage us to be better. Shouldn't this hold true for Christ as well? "If a friend is one who summons us to our best, then is not Jesus Christ our best friend and should we not think of the communion as one of the chief appeals to us to be our best? The Lord's Supper looks not back to our past with a critical eye, but to our future with a helpful one"(Maltbie Davenport Babcock, *Thoughts for Everyday Life from the Written and Spoken Words of Maltbie Davenport Babcock,* posthumously [New York: Charles Scribner's Sons, 1909], 9). Concentrating that helpful eye to the future as we meditate is an opportunity for spiritual growth (see Bryant S. Hinckley, *Sermons and Missionary Services of Melvin Joseph Ballard* [Salt Lake City: Desert Book Company, 1949], 147–57).

It is through our participation in a weekly memorial service that we qualify for the cleansing power of the Atonement of Jesus Christ. The practice of the unspoken eulogy and subsequent resolve and cleansing brings me to the very reason that I long to come to the sacrament table.

Spirit

As I REPENT DURING THE sacrament, the promise is given that His Spirit will always be with me. This is the main

reason I love to go to funerals: I long to feel the Spirit
that attends them. It is the same Spirit that is promised
in the sacrament ordinance.

There is an undeniable relationship between the
partaking of the sacrament and the companionship
of the Holy Ghost (see Dallin H. Oaks, "The Aaronic
Priesthood and the Sacrament," *Ensign,* Nov. 1998, 37).
Participating in the sacrament is a vital component to
having the Spirit. President Joseph Fielding Smith taught
that "we cannot retain the Spirit of the Lord if we do not
consistently comply with this commandment [partaking
of the sacrament]" (Joseph Fielding Smith, *Doctrines of
Salvation,* comp. Bruce R. McConkie, 3 vols. [1954–56],
2:341).

Having the constant companionship of the Holy
Ghost is the most cherished blessing of mortality.
President Wilford Woodruff called the gift of the Holy
Ghost "the greatest gift we can receive in mortality" (*The
Discourses of Wilford Woodruff,* ed. G. Homer Durham
[Salt Lake City: Bookcraft, Inc., 1990], 5). The Holy
Ghost teaches us all things and brings all things to our
remembrance (see John 14:26); unfolds the mysteries
of God (see 1 Ne. 10:19); testifies of the Son (see John
15:26; 1 Cor. 12:3); guides us into truth and shows us
things to come (see John 16:13); teaches us the truth
of all things (see Moro. 10:5); shows us all things that
are expedient (see D&C 18:18); shows us what we
should do (see 2 Ne. 32:5); is the means by which God
inspires and reveals His will to His children (see D&C
8:2–3); and enlightens our minds and fills us with joy
(see D&C 11:13). To have this great gift in our lives is
incomprehensible.

The gift of the Holy Ghost is given after baptism, but the realization of this gift comes only when we keep ourselves free from sin and only when we participate in the sacrament ordinance each Sunday. The two are inescapably linked—we must be clean in order to enjoy the gift of the Holy Ghost, and we become clean through consistently taking the sacrament.

Each Sunday we can feel the renewal of that Spirit. Elder Melvin J. Ballard said that we can feel "a spirit attending the administration of the sacrament that warms the soul from head to foot; [we] feel the wounds of the spirit being healed, and the load is lifted. Comfort and happiness come to the soul that is worthy and truly desirous of partaking of this spiritual food" ("The Sacramental Covenant," *Improvement Era,* Oct. 1919, 1027).

Spiritual Luncheon

AFTER AN LDS FUNERAL, a meal is usually provided for the family of the deceased and their guests. How wonderful it is that the Savior introduced a weekly spiritual meal for our benefit in mortality! He promised, "He that eateth this bread eateth of my body to his soul; and he that drinketh of this wine drinketh of my blood to his soul; and his soul shall never hunger nor thirst, but shall be filled" (3 Ne. 20:8). The fulfillment of that promise was then evident in the New World: "Now, when the multitude had all eaten and drunk, behold, they were filled with the Spirit" (3 Ne. 20:9).

Part of that feeling of never hungering or thirsting again is the sanctification of our souls. The English word *sacrament* literally means "to make one holy" or "to consecrate." Partaking of the spiritual food of the sacrament gives us the sustenance needed for our sanctification. Speaking of the sacrament, President Brigham Young said, "Its observance is as necessary to our salvation as any other of the ordinances and commandments that have been instituted in order that . . . people may be sanctified" (*Discourses of Brigham Young,* sel. John A. Widtsoe [Salt Lake City: Deseret Book Company, 1941], 17).

We may not always be conscious of our sanctification. However, just as I feel a void if I miss the funeral of a loved one, I also feel a loss when I miss the sacrament on a Sunday. President David O. McKay tells us that in the spiritual part of our lives the sacrament is crucial: "The operation of the law of cause and effect is as constant in the spiritual realm as it is in the physical world, and the keeping of each promise made in relation to the sacrament brings its resultant blessing, as surely as the sun brings light" (*Gospel Ideals* [Salt Lake City: Bookcraft, Inc., 1953], 73–74).

Though I cannot recall every funeral I have attended, I know that each has enhanced my soul. Likewise, I know that each weekly memorial service of the sacrament has brought a blessing. As I unite with others of my Heavenly Father's family, listen to the prayers, remember the life of my Savior, and focus on what needs to be cleansed in my life, I am filled with the Spirit and sanctified as surely as the sun brings light each day.